STILL STANDING

ONE WOMAN'S STRUGGLE WITH DIVORCE, DEPRESSION, AND BETRAYAL

VICKI FITZGERALD
M.G.CRISCI

A TRUE STORY

ORCA PUBLISHING COMPANY USA | 2020

That's Life

Doors open with adolescent innocence.
Offer flashes of yet-to-come.
Blink of an eye, shattered foundations,
Simple black and white, complex shades of grey.
Rainbow finales fade.
Diminished by darkness, battles rage,
Unimaginable collateral consequences.
Wounded, weakened, not yet expired,
Persistence rewarded.
One final Door,
Demons extricated, enemy retreats.
Sunshine reappears despite lingering doubts.
Only natural, that's life.
Hurray, still standing!

©M.G. Crisci

Dedication

To women everywhere battling to overcome life's little tests. If I can do it, so can you!

To Mum and Dad. I will make you proud. I promise. The worst is over.

Also by M.G. Crisci

7 Days in Russia
Call Sign, White Lily
Donny and Vladdy
Ergonia. Land of Giant Ants
Indiscretion
Mary Jackson Peale
Only in New York
Papa Cado
Papa Cado's Book of Wisdom
Project Zebra
Salad Oil King
Save the Last Dance
She Said. He Said.
Still Standing
This Little Piggy

Learn more at
mgcrisci.com
amazon.com/M.G.Crisci/e/B003509QRK
twitter.com/worldofmgcrisci
YouTube.com/worldofmgcrisci
Facebook.com/worldofmgcrisci

Also by Vicki FitzGerald

Briguella
Kill List
Still Standing

Learn more at
vickifitzgerald.com
Twitter.com/AuthorVickiFitz
Facebook.com/vickifitzgeraldauthor
Instagram/vickifitzgeraldauthor
YouTube.com/vickifitzgeraldauthor

Edited by Robin Friedheim and Darren Bane
Cover Design by Gold World Media
ISBN 9781456634414 (ebook)
ISBN 9781456634568 (paperback)
Manufactured in the United States of America

First Edition

1.

THE BRINY DEEP

"In the end, one needs more courage to live than to kill themselves."

— Albert Camus

2017…

How the hell did I come to be in this place?

Demons riddled my inner self. Hate, anger, bitterness, and sadness attacked relentlessly and randomly. Sledgehammers rocked my being. How to make this madness stop? I just wanted to be normal again, but I knew there was no route back to normal.

Circumstances had changed me forever. I knew I couldn't be fixed; I'd been broken too long. I was abandoned and rejected. All that remained were randomly shaped, disjointed pieces of my former self, unable, or perhaps unwilling, to form any coherence. Any logic I once possessed had been crushed beneath a mass of terribly poor choices.

I was no longer in control. I felt hollow, as though my insides had been carved. My body robotic, no longer connected to my soul, had driven me to this desolate seashore. I wanted my inner demons to be punished. No, I wanted me to be punished! The ominous dark clouds would be my final canvas.

I dragged myself toward the angry white foam. A bright full moon reflected the haggard shell of the dreadful creature I no longer recognized. I felt the sea spray whip hair strands across my face, lashing my cheeks. Again, and again.

Oddly, my leg started to vibrate. A forgotten mobile phone buried deep in my pocket began to call silently; it added to the madness of the moment. Instinctively, I knew it was John. I longed to say my final goodbye, but I knew he'd talk me out of killing myself. When things were right, he had that kind of calming presence. This time, I would have none of it. I howled wantonly, as I continued towards my destiny.

I closed my eyes and leaned forward, preparing to let go. I could feel the power of the waves smashing against the craggy cliffs. I would take one final deep breath before tumbling into the briny deep, and eternal damnation. I felt it was all I deserved.

My phone vibrated again. I hesitated for what seemed like an eternity. Why should I answer? Reluctantly, I pulled it from my pocket. It was another voicemail from John. I was torn; one side of me wanted to finish what I had begun; the other wanted to hear his voice one final time. After all we had done to each other, I still loved him.

I pressed the phone against my damp hair, closed my eyes, and listened as I entered the sea. "Vicki, please come home. We can work things out. I love you. Emily and Matthew need their mother. You are their true North…and mine."

Tears cascaded down my cheeks. I'd thrown my life away and I was full of regret, but I couldn't turn back the clock and erase it.

I stared into the dark abyss as the waves grew ever more violent. I wondered. Was redemption even remotely possible? A wave smacked me in the face. It was my answer. I began the struggle back to shore.

A few feet from the safety of dry land, my legs collapsed; I crashed to my knees. The angry waves rumbled, but I no longer wanted to die. I dug my hands into the sand and hung on for dear life. My willowy body shivered in the foreboding darkness. I could taste the wet sand fill my mouth.

Fate, or something, intervened; the waves began to recede. I gathered myself, clawed and dragged my physically and emotionally spent body to the safety of the promenade. I lay motionless as the moon reappeared from behind the clouds. My heart was pounding a thousand beats a minute.

I promised myself, "Never again." I lied.

2.

WONDERFUL WORLD

"We are not given a good life or a bad life. We are given a life. The rest is up to us."

— Ward Foley

1981…

My childhood was WONDERFUL—*not a care in the world.*

I basked in the sunshine of an innocent, untroubled childhood surrounded by laughter, hugs, and smiles, the compliments of a deliriously happy Mum and Dad, two loving grandparents who had courted from their teenage years, and an older sister, Shelly, who was my guardian and protector.

Shelly and I were treasured from the moment we were born, and I felt cherished just for being me.

Because of my support circle, I always felt safe, never afraid, and I knew if ever I fell, Mum and Dad would pick me up and mend my wounds. I was fortunate to have such a wonderful life and family.

Importantly, while I never wanted for anything, I wasn't a spoilt brat. We were taught about the values of money, dignity, and respect, values that I still hold dear—despite all that has happened.

Bonds of love are powerful, unshakeable, and should never be taken for granted.

~

My early years were spent living in a small coastal town, Portishead, where I attended St Barnabas Primary School.

I was happy, with a best friend called Amy, another close friend, Sasha, and a mate, Matthew, who lived next door. My parents would often tease me about him, playing the Boris Gardiner record (Jamaican pop reggae artist); "I Wanna Wake Up with You." I was only six.

Mum and Dad also liked to torment us. As Dad said, "It was good fun." One time, they recorded the *Jaws* soundtrack and hid speakers under our beds. Shelly and I never ran so fast in our lives! It was cruel, but they found it hilarious. It taught me that fun, laughter and love are the foundations for living.

Generally, I was well-behaved; though Amy got me in big trouble once. I was sick at school, and her mum collected me, so my mum did not have to leave work early. Amy feigned illness so she could come home, too. While we played, Amy said: "Mum and Dad have decided to repaint my bedroom on the weekend, so it's alright to draw on the walls with crayons." I was so naive at seven that I believed her. When we were done, the walls were filled with lots of lovely pictures!

While admiring our handiwork, Amy's mum opened the bedroom door. She saw the walls and went crazy. She screeched in a high-pitched voice like a madwoman and I burst into tears. I'd never felt so terrified. Truth was, I'd never ever done anything so naughty before to feel the wrath of an angry parent —I was always such a good girl. But at that moment, I was ashamed, embarrassed, and truly upset. It was a disturbing feeling, one that I'd never want to experience again.

"Vicki, you are going to be in serious trouble when your mum hears what you've done!" She paused, "Amy, how could you let Vicki scribble on the walls of your room?" I was furious that she assumed I was to blame. Amy stared at the floor, letting me take full responsibility. My heart hurt for the very first time. It was an odd sensation; one I didn't like. As a loved kid, I'd never endured emotional pain before, and I did not understand that uneasy feeling was betrayal.

"You big pig!" I retaliated. Not only was I upset, I was frightened and didn't want to be shouted at again. I pushed past her, fled down the stairs and out the back door. I ran home as fast as my little legs could carry me. I was petrified I would be in huge trouble with Mum and Dad when they came home from work.

The incident taught me an important early life lesson. *Never take someone's word as gospel truth. Always check with someone you can trust, like a Mum or Dad!*

~

Life went on. We innocently rode our bikes, went trick-or-treating on Halloween as cute witches, and raced on sleds in the snow—if it ever fell. Birthdays were filled with disco dancing and simple games like Pass the Parcel, Musical Statues, Musical Chairs, and Pin the Tail on the Donkey.

And the yummy, crumbly birthday cakes filled with jam and cream, and decorated with colorful frostings, were always made by nan Mildred. My favorite ever was a cake shaped like a pink Care Bear, complete with red liquorice paws. Nan had done me proud—it was a masterpiece.

Mum was always the Minister of Birthday Gifts. She made all the selections but as she didn't drive, she left the collecting to Dad. The year I colored Amie's walls, Dad drove hundreds of miles to buy a pink and blue doll cradle they knew I fancied. I never asked, but I always assumed Mum and Dad believed my explanation about the colored walls. *That incident taught me the power of truth; even though, as an adult, I still struggle with identifying versions of the truth.*

~

My parents worked hard. On weekends we would snuggle in bed and sing Sister Sledge: "We are family. I've got all my sisters with me." They taught me how children should be loved. So, no matter what crazy things I have done as an adult, I have always made sure to love my children in the same way. I cherish them and love them from the bottom of my heart. They are my world and I cannot imagine life without them.

15

Sundays in our household were for coming together as a family. Three generations always enjoyed a traditional British roast. Summer meals also included crisp red radishes Uncle Reg grew in his garden.

Fat Auntie Sandra (nan's sister), always provided a humorous dinner interlude. She'd perch on the same seat at the dinner table with a white starched napkin tucked over her gigantic breasts. Without fail, she'd blurt, "Albert, where is the wine?"

Gramps would pour red into the glasses dotted around the table, while everyone plated up from the antique serving dishes. Of course, the wine was always spilled or dripped onto Nan's brilliant white cloth.

"For Goodness sake Albert, why couldn't you just wait until everyone had served up. Now look at the cloth!" should be scorn. My sister and I would giggle, having already predicted the weekly wine drama.

On occasion, we would go to Auntie Sandra's house in Somerset, but my sister and I thought her house was haunted and would never go upstairs alone. It was silly. Auntie's house was Victorian, but there certainly were no ghosts. The fact was, she rarely put the heating on, so the house was always freezing, which we mistook for creepy. Still, we enjoyed delicious roasts and playing solitaire marbles while there.

~

While we weren't rich, Dad and Mum made sure they saved money for a nice annual family vacation. Summers usually meant seaside caravan holidays to Devon and Cornwall, where Shelly and I wore matching frilly bikinis, tassel beach dresses, jelly shoes, and cool fancy-dress costumes that Dad designed for the clubhouse competitions.

As we got older, we began to venture abroad, often joined by Nan and Gramps, to beautiful resorts in Menorca, Cyprus, Crete, and France. I felt like the luckiest kid in the world. During the day, we'd go rock climbing with Dad, build elaborate sandcastles and speedboats, and get buried in the sand on the beach. Dad used to joke, "Vicki, you are very good at burying men." Neither he nor I knew how right he was at the time.

Evenings were reserved for visiting Greek tavernas. Mum and Dad's favorite spot in Limassol, Cyprus, was the Blue Island restaurant, where food always took second place to dance. Male dancers wore traditional pleated skirts, white shirts, black satin waist sashes, and cute shoes with pompons. I was fascinated. Everyone would dance on tables, in the street, balance glasses on the dancers' heads, and even set fire to newspapers tucked into their skirts as they danced! The Blue Island is where I developed my lifelong love affair with dancing. Dancing makes me laugh and feel good, even during the darkest moments.

Family holidays taught me that laughter should always be part of life, something I've forgotten at points in my life. Mum and Dad also instilled us with three other values that I hold dear:

- *Family is everything, especially respect for your elders.*
- *Kindness matters, so always be courteous.*
- *Recognize that that fear is an illusion, so never feel afraid.*

~

My first personal crisis occurred at the age of seven, when we moved to a new house in Weston-super-Mare, a traditional seaside town, to be closer to Nan and Gramps.

Mum transferred her job in a Portishead warehouse to the Weston branch, much closer to her parents, whom she loved dearly. At first blush, the move made great sense. The new house was bigger, and the garden was quite substantial. Dad planted colorful Petunias, Fuchsia, Hydrangeas, and Begonias and Mum loved to potter around and see the fruits of their labor.

We had fun living by the beach with donkeys and Punch and Judy puppet shows. Weston also has a big pier with amusements and rides, and at the time, the Tropicana, a huge lido (public open-air swimming pool) with a wave machine and pineapple-shaped water chutes. It was THE place to be and the most fun you could ever have.

The one thing Weston didn't have were friends for me. Even though we were less than an hour from Portishead, I had to start all over, a frightening thought when you're young. But my sister Shelly was always there, even though she teased me unmercifully.

For the first weeks after the move, I remained at my current school, St Barnabas, while the details of my transfer to my new school, Becket, were finalized. One day, I waited at the St Barnabas school steps for what seemed like hours with the lollipop lady (road crossing attendant), crying my eyes out—every other child had been collected except me.

My mind wandered to thoughts of Shelly telling me, "I'm Mum and Dad's favorite; they love me more than you." Shelly also insisted, "Vicki, you're adopted. That's why there are hardly any baby pictures of you!" I *thought* it wasn't true, Mum always told Shelly to stop being naughty, but I never forgot. The longer I waited with the lollipop lady, the more I wondered; was Shelly right? Did Mum and Dad not want me anymore? I was a kid after all and believed everything I was told.

As it turned out, my "dreadful concern" was simply a case of crossed wires. Mum thought Gramps was going to pick me up that day; she got her days mixed up.

So, to everyone who blurts in jest—think about the receiving party. Unintended, hurtful comments can last far longer than well-intentioned compliments.

~

When the time came to start at Becket, my worries about new friends quickly dissipated. It was there I received my first handmade Valentine's Card and experienced another new sensation; romance.

His name was Lee. We were in the same class, and he'd left the card in my school drawer. When I opened it, I could feel his smile. My heart raced and my cheeks blushed for the first time. It was a warm, fuzzy feeling that was exciting but also embarrassing. I quickly hid the card in my school bag.

We *never* spoke about it! I guess at the age of nine I was more interested in playing with Barbie dolls than making boys laugh and cry, sometimes all at once!

~

One of my most vivid memories in our new home was Shelly's brazen attempts at mischief. Once, she locked me in a shed at a garden center and told Mum and Dad that she had not seen me. I was locked inside for about an hour, crying and utterly terrified, before I was found. Shelly feigned surprise, pretending she knew nothing of my incarceration.

There was also the Nightmare on Elm Street incident. Our uncle was watching the movie at Nan's house. We snuck in to see a bit of the film. We were shocked to see a girl with blonde hair flying around the ceiling covered in blood. Freddy Krueger had sliced her open with his knives. I felt sick and trembled all over, experiencing real fear for the first time. I was absolutely petrified and haunted by the graphic images.

Neither of us could sleep that night. We were both scared, even though Shelly pretended she wasn't. Shelly crept into my room and whispered, "Don't worry, I've worked it out. The blonde girl died first, so if Freddy comes, he'll kill you before me." (I was a natural blonde as a kid). I cried myself to sleep.

The most mischievous and looking back as an adult, the funniest stunt Shelly played was with one of my dolls after we had watched the horror movie, *Child's Play*.

Admittedly, the doll did look like the killer Chucky doll from the film. She obtained a kitchen knife, cello-taped it to the doll's hand, and put it in my bed under the duvet. I screamed until my lungs were empty. Fear was a feeling that I didn't enjoy, and hoped in adult life, I'd never have to experience it. I was wrong.

3.

FIRST DANCE

"Heroes are ordinary people who make themselves extraordinary."

– Gerard Way

1987...

When you are a kid, there is always that one person you look up to, aside from your loving parents. Mine was Gramps Albert.

I'm sure every granddaughter puts their grandfather on a pedestal, but my Gramps was truly special in every way.

Picture little Sophie in Roald Dahl's novel, The Big Friendly Giant—a girl who believes she can save the world with the benevolent BFG.

Gramps was no BFG, but he was a dapper man with a heart bigger than the universe, a smile that glistened, and a sense of humor that knew no bounds.

"Come here, my angel, sit on my knee," Gramps always insisted whenever I went to visit.

I would run for cuddles in his armchair in front of the fire, or as he sat on the kitchen stool. I'd snuggle into his warm woolen V-neck jumper that smelt of Old Spice. His love made me feel all was right with the world, and always would be. He taught me the importance of unconditional love.

Gramps took pride in his appearance. I can still picture him standing in front of the kitchen wall mirror, combing his hair carefully into place—a man of pride. "It doesn't cost much to look your best, just a few minutes of your time, and a little attention to detail." Gramps passed his appearance-consciousness onto me; I've always tried to look my best, dress smart, and be pristine for any occasion.

~

Gramps immensely enjoyed party games like Bingo, Admiral Nelson, and the £1 game that allowed him to indulge his charming sense of humor. During Admiral Nelson, participants were blindfolded and told they were meeting the great war hero himself. Their hand was guided to a leg, stopping at the knee, and told dynamite caused its loss, the same with an arm to an elbow, which was lost in a duel.

Finally, he would say that, at the Battle of Waterloo, his right eye was lost. Our finger was shoved into an orange to mimic an eye socket!

Trust me, it was very convincing, as was the belief that we would keep the £1 at the bottom of a bowl if we could grab it in one attempt.

Of course, while blindfolded, the bowl would be swapped for the turkey's giblets and gravy—yuck! Those games taught me a new feeling; repulsion. But I did enjoy being teased.

Gramps' all-time favorite game was the "dribbling cup." Unbeknown to me, at seven, he took a drinking glass with an etched design and drilled some tiny holes that were virtually invisible. The idea was that when you tried to drink from it; the liquid would spill everywhere.

"My glass is broken!" I cried, embarrassed.

"Don't be silly. You're just dribbling. Turn the glass to the other side," Gramps answered, straight-faced.

I took another sip and another. Each time, the drink would spill over my chin. So, everybody in the room was having a chuckle at my expense. When he saw I was at my wits' end, he revealed the trick and a little bit of wisdom. "Life is for living and laughing," he said. I adored that he wanted to have fun with me.

Somewhere along the way, I began to take life too seriously. I forgot to laugh at my silly little foibles. As you'll soon discover, I've strayed far from Gramps' advice. The good news is I now recognize that.

~

As a kid, I always looked forward to the family summer holidays with Nan and Gramps, which usually coincided with his birthday on June 27. Gramps would swap his usual smart attire for a polo shirt and shorts and down cold Carlsberg pints in the scorching sunshine with Dad. Then there were the wine tasting trips where there was no limit. Bottle after bottle was opened. Watching adults get sloshed then walk in the heat clinking bottles like teenagers, amused Shelly and me.

~

My most memorable Gramps' moment—one that still brings a tear to my eye—was him teaching me to waltz.

I was about eight at the time. We danced at Gramps' Ruby wedding party (40 years). I can still picture the smile on his face. My hair was curled, and I wore a green and black glitter taffeta dress and black patent shoes. He smiled, took my hand, and we stepped onto the dance floor beneath a large mirror disco ball. I was nervous and self-conscious. In fact, I was totally clueless. I didn't know what a Waltz was, let alone, the dance steps.

"It's easy, just follow my lead," Gramps said.

Then he took me in his arms, and we danced. It was magical. All was right with the world. Gramps made me feel like a special princess and his smile, as we glided across the dance floor, melted my heart. I wanted the moment to last forever!

~

Gramps always made me believe there was nothing I couldn't do or achieve. The speech he gave at my 18th birthday said it all.

"I could pay tribute to Vicki's many gifts—her appearance, her charm, and her caring attitude towards others," he said, "but I'm sure most of you know about those.

"I'd like to recognize her outstanding academic achievements at school and her first-class reports since starting technical college.

"In addition to her studies, Vicki has undertaken part-time jobs, and her employers have all spoken very highly of her.

"Finally, I'd like to wish her well and success in her ambitions and aspirations for university, which she will start later this year.

"Please raise a toast to my dear sweet granddaughter!"

That autumn (fall), I became the first person in the family to go to university. I packed my belongings, left home, said a tearful goodbye, and entered an exciting new life chapter.

As he and I hugged, he whispered, "Make Gramps proud." We both had tears in our eyes. All I ever wanted to do was to make him proud, and I did for a very long time. God, I idolized him!

Sadly, Gramps passed away in 2010 at the age of 72, after a short, sudden illness. He deserved to live far longer. Both Auntie Sandra and Uncle Reg had died during my childhood, but I did not recall how it felt. Losing Gramps was an entirely different matter. It was traumatic. It felt as though someone had punched a fist through my chest and torn my heart out with their bare hands. That was the first time my body and mind was consumed by grief and despair. I'd lost a part of me and life would never ever be the same again.

One of the biggest regrets in my life to date is I never got to dance at my wedding with Gramps. If only I could go back in time and relieve that night; Waltz as we'd done in the past. His early departure had a traumatic effect on my life for years to come. I'm still angry and bitter with the angels who stole my Gramps from me. I'll never get over it.

Gramps' early demise taught me that sometimes life just happens. We cannot change fate. So, when we lose those we love and cherish long before their time, some of us learn to weather life's inevitable storms, while some of us get terribly lost in the very same storms.

4.

MY PORKY PIE

"The real history of consciousness starts with one's
first lie."

– Joseph Brodsky

1988...

*My first porky pie (innocent fib) was never intended to hurt
anyone's feelings. I was just the new girl at a new school, and I wanted
to be liked.*

It was more like Shelly's and my "little secret." Ironically, it
was the first of many lies to come!

Becket Primary had a non-school-uniform policy. We could
wear whatever we wanted. Cool, hey? Except Mum dressed us
identically. Don't get me wrong; we were the best-dressed kids, in
posh embroidery Anglaise dresses with satin ribbon bows
around our waists.

You name it, we wore it, and yes, we looked beautiful, but we
hated being matching. Shelly, two years older, was more annoyed
than me. One day she came up with a rather creative solution:
"It's simple," explained Shelly, "we just tuck some spare clothes
into our bags and change in the garages before we head to
school!"

"What, the block of public garages behind other people's
homes?"

"Yeah!"

"Suppose someone sees us changing? Or Mum walks past
during break time and notices we have changed?" I worried.

"It will be fine," responded Shelly. "Plus, Mum never walks
past the school!"

It was naughty betraying Mum, but I wanted to look cool in class. Imagine, I could wear what I wanted. My first selection was a pair of baby blue callots shorts (ones that look like a skirt) and a matching top that tied in the front. Since I was worried Mum would notice a lot of clothes were missing, I wore the same outfit every day that first week. I'm sure the teachers noticed, but they never said a thing.

As a kid, there would be many more fibs and cover-ups: spilling nail polish on the sofa, breaking a china basket ornament and gluing it back together with toothpaste, and searching the house top to bottom in the weeks before Christmas to find our presents.

As a teen, the Porky Pies grew larger: bowling nights with friends meant underage drinking at local discos and sneaking out on holiday in Turkey to meet up with a hot boy—I'll come to that little escapade later.

I became pretty good at justifying my little lies. I rationalized they didn't really hurt anybody, and my friends were doing the same thing!

As I was to learn painfully, *lies do matter. When someone you love lies to you, it hurts. Equally, when you lie and it hurts someone you love, it's sickening.* It might even make you a little irrational, which is what happened to me.

~

Primary school flew by. I loved to read and quickly worked my way through to higher levels. My favorite books were Roald Dahl's and Frances Hodgson Burnett's, The Secret Garden.

I formed a love of both writing and reading and even created a newspaper, *The Gazette*. I'd sit for hours writing articles.

The only bad memory occurred when I was about 11. An Ouija board had been taken to school by a scary shaggy-haired girl who claimed the board allowed her to contact the spirit world.

I told her she was full of you-know-what. "Watch," she said, "I have asked an evil spirit to place a curse on anyone with a surname that begins with the letter F." She then pointed at my two friends and me. "That means you, you, and you."

We were terrified! I remember going home and shaking like a leaf while crying against Mum's chest. It was a different type of fear because I couldn't control what wasn't there; ghosts. I feared I'd be haunted by demons forever. Maybe I am and that's what has led to poor, regrettable life choices. Who knows?

~

Secondary school was daunting. I was small and thin as a stick. My sister Shelly told her friends that Mum and Dad named me *Cauli Flower* (cauliflower). My maiden surname was Flowers!).

The kids would always find ways to tease me. One looked at me and said, "Vicki, what's that string hanging from your skirt?" Another would respond, "Oh, that's your legs!" Such comments hurt and messed with my self-esteem. They left invisible bruises on my skin which have stayed on me into adulthood. I began to realise that our own actions, and that of others, can be traumatizing.

Summer camp arrived; it was humiliating. I was 11-years-old, but I hadn't developed like the other girls. We'd been asked to undress and use communal showers. I'd never taken my clothes off in front of anyone other than my mum! I was a prude and very self-conscious. I simply did not want to do it but was made to face the indignity, which in turn, crushed any confidence I had left.

"Vicki has no boobs or pubes!" Becky declared loudly on the school bus, mocking my figure to the boys while proudly showing off her push-up bra, as though she was the Queen Bee.

I slid down in my chair, cringing, and cried all the way home. I wanted the floor to crumble and swallow me up whole. It was the first time I'd ever felt humiliation and it broke me.

After that, I became timid and feared further hurtful comments. They came, of course; people can be cruel. One memory, that sticks above all others, was being told I was fat. (I weighed 5 kilos and was pencil thin.) The boy was joking, but I went home and swallowed laxatives to make myself thinner!

Despite my shyness, I was welcomed into the cool circle. People found me humorous, and I was invited to everything.

Boys and girls started to date; well, hanging out with each other on their bikes after school if that's what you would class as dating; at 11 or 12. I didn't want to be left out, so I agreed to go on a date with Ed. I thought having a boyfriend would boost my confidence. We had our first kiss on the tennis courts. It was sloppy, and I wanted to be sick.

Nothing against him, I just wasn't ready to French Kiss. Hence, we lasted only a few days, and I didn't rush out for a new boyfriend.

~

Aged 13, feeling more mature and ready to date for real this time, I asked out James, a boy in the school year below me.

He was cute, with dark hair, blue eyes, and dimples when he smiled. He reminded me of *Boyzone's,* Stephen Gatley; he was hot!

James said, "yes." We'd go out on our bikes or to the park. We held hands and kissed a couple of times. We were both shy, and I don't even recall him ever trying to grab my rear while kissing me. Pure innocence was the extent of a childhood romance in those days.

I liked him; he was funny. But out of the blue, he dealt a blow (delivered some bad news), "I'm sorry, but I'm leaving our school to go to Cannington, an agricultural school," he said, a tinge of sadness in his voice.

James' family owned a farm; he would continue their legacy and needed to switch to a farming school to learn the ropes.

Feeling like I would never see him, given he lived in Banwell village, a few miles away, I cruelly dumped him. We were at my mum's house when James' best friend, Toby, suddenly turned on the CD player, playing break up songs—somehow, he knew I was about to tell James "sayonara"—cheers, Toby!

I can't remember my exact words; after all, I was only 13, but I did let him down gently. Hurting him felt dreadful, I felt nauseous and cruel. Despite me ending the young romance, I felt my heart ache for the first time—a dreadful feeling. I think he was gutted; I was older and made him look cool.

Toby found the whole thing hilarious, seeing his best mate get dumped by a girl. I suppose *I learned that young boys could be very childish and were far less mature than us girls!*

~

A year or so later, I'd become best friends with a humorous classmate named Stephen. He had a nice smile and dark hair but was different from James and Ed.

We'd sit by each other in classes. At the end of school, Stephen was voted the funniest male, and I was voted the funniest girl. Humour was our connection. He loved my stupid impressions, especially of the 90s Dime bar TV commercial featuring an unsophisticated countryman, saying in a West Country (regional Somerset accent): *"I likes Armadillos, smooth on the inside, crunchy on the outside."*

One day he asked me out. He said we should be boyfriend and girlfriend, seeing as we got on like a house on fire (got on well). The problem was we had become such good friends, dating felt odd. We kissed, laughed, and went back to being mates. Eventually, Stephen married another school friend, Anya, and they had two kids. But he, she and I remain Facebook friends to this day.

~

As I grew up doing my "boy thing," flitting from friendships to dates, the time came when I embarked on my first holiday romance.

Family holidays became a bit more adventurous. I have vivid memories of our first trip to Turkey. The traditions and customs were different from any other country I'd ever visited.

We bathed in the unofficial eighth wonder of the world, Pamukkale thermal pools. When we finished, I remember vividly how the ruddy, dark-skinned Turkish men would flock to touch my unusual blonde hair, as if I was an angelic icon. (All the Turkish girls I met had dark brown or black hair.)

My parents were offered 50 camels and a very nice yacht to buy me. Dad played along for a bit. I was terrified Mum and Dad would eventually agree. Fortunately, they did not. Thank you, Mum and Dad.

Other than fear of being sold, I enjoyed wonderful experiences in Turkey: holding a giant swordfish, then eating it, taking camel rides, and being soaped up in a Turkish bath which felt like laying on a marble mortuary slab covered in bubbles, then sliding around like a wet fish.

~

The holiday (vacation) also contained its fair share of "naughty" Porkie Pie moments. One of the most memorable, which I mentioned earlier, was when my sister Shelly and I told Mum and Dad we were tired and going to retire a bit early. I sensed Dad thought it was a bit strange since we hadn't done much all day besides lunch and sunbathe on the beach. But he said nothing.

I was all in because I wanted to see Aaron again—a cool guy with floppy hair and muscular build who, a day earlier, had chatted me up at the bar. He picked me over Shelly, who was two years older (the same age as Aaron) and looked a lot sexier.

I liked the plans but had reservations. Lying and betrayal sat heavily on my chest, but I also wanted to be daring. "Mum and

Dad are right next door. How are we ever going to get past them because our door creaks like crazy?"

"Out the window, of course!"

Minutes later, my butt was sticking out of the window, as Shelly waited so that we could head up the path.

We didn't know Mum and Dad had decided to go for a romantic walk in the moonlight.

"Where do you think you're going?" boomed my father's familiar voice. Red-faced, stomach knotted, with no excuse for dangling half in, half out, we were marched straight back to bed.

Despite that little setback, Aaron and I did manage to meet up a night or two later. He walked me down to the beach, and we kissed beneath the stars. He was a delightful kisser. He also convinced me to puff on my first cigarette afterwards. I didn't like the taste of cigarettes and never smoked again. But kissing was another matter!

It was also super-cool showing my friends photos of my "older" holiday romance hunk. That first kiss with an 'older guy' did wonders for my confidence. I wasn't undesirable after all. I could be admired by gorgeous boys and the feeling was both exciting and terrifying.

5.

NICE TUSH

"You should be kissed often and by someone who knows how."

– Margaret Mitchell

1996…

As a teenager, with newfound confidence, I grew up fast. Although some people—like Mum, Dad, and Shelly—would argue I was growing up too quickly.

After returning from the Turkish summer holiday, I sneaked a bottle of a heavy-duty 80-proof mint liquor into my suitcase. I took it to my friend Liz's house party and got drunk for the first time. As naïve kids, we didn't realize the strength of the liquor and drank it in coffee mugs. First, I had a fun buzz; then, people started to look fuzzy, then I had no idea what I was doing.

Next thing I knew, my best friend Lily said, "Your dad is at the front door to pick you up. We giggled like two silly kids—which we were.

Lily then passed out on the kitchen floor!

I tried to act sober as I headed to Dad, but I fell straight through the front door.

Dad, smirking, didn't let on. He caught me in his loving arms, and asked, "Where's Lily?

"Asleep on the kitchen floor," I answered calmly, as though it were the most natural thing in the world to sleep on the floor tiles.

"Is she okay?" he asked, looking rather worried.

"She's fine. Just messing around!"

"Okay," nodded Dad.

The ride home was eerily silent. I assumed the worst was to come when Dad told Mum. But, to my surprise, there was not a word. The next morning Dad woke me up with a gentle tug. "Time for work." (Lily and I had jobs as ice cream sellers in beach huts in the school holidays, for £15 a day, a huge sum for us). So, I dragged myself down to the Weston seafront boardwalk with my first hangover. I noticed Dad laughing out of the corner of his face as I struggled to the door; I think he rather enjoyed my first hangover. That first day after my first hangover still lingers: schmoozing customers and selling Mr. Whippy ice creams and candy floss in the hot sun.

~

During my early teen years, Lily and I realized we liked boys, loved to dance, and were not shy about drinking alcopops, like all our friends.

One day, two handsome new boys arrived at school, a Brit named Ian and a Canadian named Jeff. Jeff had this unusual international accent, which made him super cool. My girlfriends drooled. Everyone wanted to hang out with them. All the girls fancied him and tried to let him know. Jeff split time between his parents in the UK and Canada.

By contrast, Ian and his family had moved down from Manchester and spoke with a northern accent. His mum was lovely and let him have cool parties where booze was allowed! I made sure to get myself invited, and we all drank bottles of alcopops, Hooch, and Smirnoff Ice. Those parties were a blast.

At those social gatherings, Jeff introduced us to Thug Bones N Harmony's, *Crossroads*. The song became a party anthem, as did Tupac's *Changes*, Montell Jordan's, *This is How We Do It*, and Puff Daddy's, *I'll be Missing You*.

~

One of Ian's parties did get me into trouble.

I had my first fondle with the then boy of my dreams, David. He was gorgeous, with intoxicating dimples, a charming smile, and perfect pearly-white teeth. Before that night, he'd been dating another good friend, Katherine. But at Ian's party he decided he wanted to get close to me instead. I guess it wasn't the right thing to do, sloppy seconds and all that, but it wasn't the first—or the last time—I would make a foolish choice.

David and I slipped into the night when no one was looking. We kissed under a full moon, and he tenderly caressed me over my clothes. The incident was kind of exciting for a young teenager, so I decided to put all the details in my diary. Mum accidentally discovered the darn thing under the bed whilst she was cleaning. She was appalled at the revelation. "I can't believe you would write this!"

I responded, "I can't believe you would spy on my personal life." Not the best retort. Mum grounded me immediately and indefinitely!

~

I'm now 15, hanging out with the cool kids and going to Ian's awesome parties. There was no romance between Ian and me—we were just good friends and still are to this day.

Suddenly, Ricky, the school's "bad boy," started chasing me.

Ricky was one tough lad. He was the self-proclaimed leader of the "naughty gang," smoked like a chimney under the subway, and skipped classes whenever he wanted. But nobody said anything to anybody.

For some random reason I'd caught his eye, despite my bad perm and braces.

"We should go out together," he said in the school playground.

"Sorry, I'm not interested," I replied. I found Ricky intimidating and not the least bit attractive. He could have gone out with any girl he wanted; most would have jumped at the chance. Oddly, the more I rejected his advances, the more determined he became.

I didn't know what to do; my friends convinced me I'd made the right decision—bad boys are just plain bad, and I should steer clear. My school head of year, Mr. T, must have heard of Ricky's obsession. He said in a scribbled note, "Vicki, you're too good for him." He added, in the written passage of my leavers' book, something that would probably get him fired today.

"You've blossomed from a caterpillar into a beautiful butterfly with quite a nice tush (bottom), too."

At the time, I thought nothing of it; I found his comment amusing. I've since wondered what attracted an intelligent male educator to the nice tush of a 15-year-old?

~

A girl, two years above us, named Vicky (same name, different spelling), who really wanted to go out with Ricky, became insanely jealous. She started calling me "Little Miss Plain Jane" in the school halls.

I quickly learned that jealousy could make people work in mysterious ways! Vicky went from taunting to bullying to calling me all kinds of nasty names and tripping me up in the school halls.

It went on for months. I was terrified. It got to the point that I felt afraid to go to school because the crazy Vicky frightened me.

The ordeal came to a head at a school disco. I was dancing to Mark Morrison's classic, *Return of the Mack*, when Vicky wrapped her hands around my throat, trying to strangle me. "If you don't leave him alone, I'll kill you."

Her actions sparked a raging fire I didn't know existed. I lashed out, pushing her back in defence. Vicky was shocked that I'd fought back and walked off.

Ironically THAT Vicky taught THIS Vicki another valuable life lesson. *Don't let the fear of something paralyze you; always stand up for what you believe.* I also learned something else: bullies are cowards. The Vicky incident made me stronger as a person. I never allowed anyone to push me around afterwards—until I met the devil.

6.

MY FIRST LOVE

"When I saw you, I fell in love, and you smiled because
you knew."

– Arrigo Boito

1997…

*Fake college ID's and some partying led to a bloody foot and
prince charming coming to the rescue.*

I had two passions as a high school teenager; pass my school
GCSE (a qualification taken by school students aged 14–16, at a
level below A level) exams and continue to rock socially with
sleepovers at my friend Lily's house and our bowling nights.

Lily's mum would drop us at the bowling alley, dressed in
high heels, lips smeared with Rimmel Heather Shimmer glossy
lipstick, and oozing CK One perfume, which reeked of orange,
mandarin, papaya, bergamot, lemon, jasmine, nutmeg, and rose.

As soon as Lily's mum was out of sight, we would head for
our favorite local seafront bars and clubs: Mr. Bees, Steamrock,
and Montana's.

Lily's mum never said a word about our bowling alley dress-
ups. I assume she was either naïve or just decided to turn a blind
eye—more likely the latter. Even the club bouncers *appeared* to
fall for our glamorous makeovers and phony ID's.

Our goal was to have a good time and spend no more than
£20 for drinks and cloakroom. One summer night, we had been
dancing up a storm in Montana's to 90s classics; Mouse T, *I'm
Horny,* Ultra Natee, *I'm Free,* and The Weather Girls, *It's Raining
Men.*

Someone accidentally dropped a glass on the dance floor and cut my foot open. I was oozing blood but couldn't get into the ladies' room because of the horrendous queue.

That's how I met Will.

Will, whom I'd never seen before, was also at the club that night. He must have seen me bleeding and panicking because he arrived armed with a ton of tissues.

"Here, let me help you," he said, offering a warm smile.

Gently, he cleaned up my foot and reassured me that I would be okay. He was utterly charming, and I felt butterflies in my tummy. I didn't want him to leave, so I played the damsel-in-distress. It worked, we sat and talked for hours in a dimly lit booth, since dancing was out of the question.

The very next day, I was back working at the beach hut. Will again appeared like magic! I was surprised but pleased, very pleased. I must have mentioned where I worked during our chat.

"I just wanted to check on my patient," he smiled. That's when my heart skipped a beat for the first time.

The gesture was romantic, his smile and charm even more so. I thought to myself, "Goodness, the man is two years older, studying at college, and interested in little old me!"

I felt like the cat who got the cream. Will was more than a fun guy with piercing blue eyes and a fabulous laugh. He owned a cool car—a gold Ford Escort. (Remember I was a teenager.)

After a few dates, Will was convinced we had a special connection, and he asked me to be his "exclusive" girlfriend. I paused for two seconds and then said yes! He was over the moon.

And, so was I!

~

Mum and Dad adored Will; he became part of the family, always greeting Mum by a nickname; "Hey, Boss!" Mum found it funny, and I guess it added to his charm. I dated him through college while studying A-level qualifications and gaining my driving license.

I ended up gaining a part-time job with Will in Marks & Spencer in the food department. He would pick me up at 6.30 am—talk about dedication.

"Watch for the spiders in the bananas," he would tease me. It would freak me out. I didn't want to get bitten by a huge spider.

We became inseparable; I knew I had fallen in love for the very first time.

Will was perfect in every imaginable way. And everybody called us the perfect couple. Will was also the first man I was ever intimate with. When his soft hands caressed my skin, it felt electrifying, sending tingles all over my body. He was gentle and slow, and I didn't feel at all afraid.

I knew that I could trust him, and I was happy that I'd reserved my 'first time' for someone truly special. Though, I wasn't overly impressed by the uncomfortable ordeal.

Before long, I turned 18. I celebrated with a party and wore an electric blue dress and tiara and danced on the table with all my friends to Britney Spears, *Baby One More Time*.

I could see from the sheer volume of friends and family who attended that I was loved. I was a very lucky girl.

At Christmas, I opened a huge box. It was packed with gym weight discs and box after box inside to trick me.

When I finally discovered the gift, it was a solitaire diamond ring. It was special, but Will never actually popped the question. Still, I knew that I meant the world to him.

~

My goal was simple. I'd passed my A-levels at Bridgwater College and wanted to go to university in Cardiff. But I missed my first choice by a mere two points. I was beyond devastated and cried for hours.

I felt I had failed myself and my parents. But I enrolled at my second choice—Southampton Institute, to study a BA (Hons) in Journalism.

At the time, I had no idea that fate (and distance) would alter my destiny. As I left for university, I was a confident young woman with hopes, aspirations, and dreams of fairy-tale endings. Mum and Dad, Gramps and Nan had it all; I was confident, so would I. The only downside was that Southampton meant I would be further away from Will.

~

Southampton was a huge city, two and a half hours away, and I felt petrified at the thought of being so far from home.

As my leaving day came closer, Will became quiet and showed little interest in my university preparations. I genuinely believed it was because he was sad. Will promised we could make long-distance work, though he had graduated from college and was a highflyer for British Airways as an on-call tech engineer. I ventured off. I cried my eyes out when my parents left me in my new Halls of Residence. I was a capable young woman, but scared.

Fortunately, I shared an 11-bed dorm with some wonderful girls, many who became friends, some best friends for life.

We frequently partied, played funny games and silly dares (naughty challenges). We also danced up a storm in Ikon and Diva nightclub. But we also found time to shop and study.

I must have picked up on my sister's tricks too and my new university friend, Mary, was gullible, so I had some fun.

I'm not sure which was the cruelest—the letter from the Dean (principal) kicking her out of halls or the prank Halloween calls.

Mary's boyfriend used to stay over in the halls. I scanned in the university logo and wrote a letter informing Mary she was expelled and kicked out for allowing him to stay.

"What am I going to tell my parents?" she sobbed.

"I'm not sure, but I'm sure they will forgive you," I comforted.

She cried for at least half an hour before I confessed to my crime and apologized for being so cruel. I did take it too far!

Then there were the scary Halloween calls, my voice saying, "I'm watching you." Mary burst into my room. "I know it's you!"

I played dumb, roped in another pal to take my role, then followed her back to her room. The phone rang again, "I'm watching you!" When she saw the caller wasn't me, she freaked out. Boy, I was mean, but we became best friends, and she still loves me.

~

University was like nothing I'd known. I'd been used to Mum doing all my cooking and cleaning. Now, all I had were recipe cards.

I made it work. I studied, transferred my job at Marks & Spencer, and worked part-time around my degree to earn a wage. This time in ladies' fashion, so there was no chance of a creepy spider encounter.

Will would visit. I'd grow excited at his arrival for a weekend, but it seemed like every visit was cut short by a work emergency call. At first, I tried to deal with the problem. But this behavior continued for months; it drove a huge wedge between us.

I suppose it also changed how I felt about Will. I felt neglected. He had made his choice: HIS work was more important than US.

The constant disappointment taught me something else—I was only 19. Perhaps, I should be young and carefree like other girls, not tied down. I was confused. But the confusion quickly turned to disillusionment.

One weekend I'd visited Will at his flat in Weston and found a long dark hair in his bed. I felt as though my heart had been torn from my chest.

"What the hell is this? Have you slept with another girl?" I yelled.

"No! Of course not! I wouldn't. I don't know how it got there!"

Since I was a mirror image of Claire Richards, the blonde, wild and crazy lead singer of the popular pop group Steps, my mind imagined all sorts of dubious activities.

I went a bit crazy. Will provided some fabricated story.

"I had a party. Loads of people stayed over. I slept on the sofa. I've no idea whose hair it is, but I didn't cheat on you. I wouldn't."

Naively, I *tried* to believe him, because I wanted his explanation to be the truth. Of all the boys I'd known, Will was my childhood sweetheart and my one true love.

Besides, Will had *always* told me the truth, even when it wasn't convenient.

Like the time my friend Lily and I had drifted apart. I'd assumed, like Will, that she was upset that I was leaving her behind to attend university.

In the months before I'd left, we were all on a night out in town. Katherine and I shared a taxi home, Will and Lily lived in town.

Lily asked him to walk her home since she didn't want to walk the dark streets alone. Will obliged. According to Will, Lily tried to kiss him along the way, and he turned down her advances.

When Will told me, I was furious! Lily had tried to kiss her friend's boyfriend! How could she betray me like that? Was Will's version of the truth what happened? I'll never know.

I couldn't erase the possibility of Will sleeping with another girl from my mind. And I was too proud to ask Lily.

~

After the hair incident, I returned to university a different person. Could I ever completely trust Will again? I also knew I was young, full of life, and had a lot to offer the right someone.

It was also that clear the heartstrings connecting me, and Will were severing. I confided in Mum that I was at the end of my rope. She told me, "Don't do anything rash," and to think things over during the Christmas holidays. She adored Will.

I came home and completed the family festivities: traditional turkey with all the trimmings. The unsuspecting Will enjoyed our time together like nothing ever happened.

He even gave me a pair of earrings as a Christmas present. I'd felt sick opening them. They were gold knot studs – timeless classics, but I found them old fashioned. Maybe he didn't know me at all?

A few days later, into the New Year, I broke his heart. We were tucked away in a bar, Will was his confident self, I'd painted on a smile, but underneath I was a quivering wreck with clammy hands.

I grew some balls and told him to his face, "I'm sorry Will, I can't do this anymore. The long distance just isn't working." I barely saw him anymore because of his job and told him that we should go our separate ways. He cried, so did I.

Mum and Dad were gutted. They loved Will; he had been part of our family for years. I suppose they felt they'd lost a future son-in-law. "Are you sure you've made the right decision?" Mum quizzed.

"I don't know," I answered sheepishly. I never confided about the hair. I didn't want Mum to think badly of Will—she loved him.

I believe, if circumstances had been different, and I *might* have gone to Cardiff, we would have married one day.

It's also entirely possible that Will and I were just not meant to be.

7.
CRAZY JACK

"You have to keep breaking your heart until it opens."
— Rumi

2000…

Just when my heart had been broken, along came crazy Jack to liven up my life at university.

For some reason, finding that *next to perfect guy* has never been a problem with me. My girlfriends tease and say that I have a certain charismatic charm that attracts both nice guys and weirdos, but sometimes I have trouble distinguishing between the two.

Most men I've met would probably describe me a bit differently. They would say I have "come-to-bed eyes." I find that troubling since it sounds tawdry and cheap, but apparently, that vibe is one of my demons.

In all honesty, I'm neither promiscuous nor am I a one-night stand. I want to be loved in the right way by the right man.

~

As Will became a distant memory, I decided it was time to move on and have a few girls' nights out. University nights were meant to be filled with laughter and dancing, and I was good at both.

During one of those evenings, I ran into a handsome guy called Jack, who had gelled black hair, at The Beach nightclub in Southampton. He oozed fun, busted some crazy moves on the dance floor, and, like me, loved to laugh. In other words, he ticked all my boxes.

We met a few times, danced up a storm to Garage music, and kissed passionately. Jack wasn't a student, he was an unpolished "townie" (non-student) who wanted to live the life I was living, so I welcomed him into my circle.

I trusted him; he always had my back. We had a lot of fun together, but I knew as time progressed that we could never be anything serious. He was too much of a clown and quite reckless.

I remember the day my housemates and I decided to bake a hash cake. Jack said he'd acquire the cannabis, so we all chipped in. We had to try it once in our lives. By the time we finished baking, we had this sticky green sugar-laden pound cake.

"Looks a little weird," said Jack. "Better let me taste it first." And, so, he did. "It tastes pretty good!" smiled Jack, surprised. We all then devoured the whole thing. We didn't realize we had put about four times too much cannabis into the mix. Everyone began to freak out, since we were completely stoned and passed out.

When we woke 24 hours later, I realized I had missed one of my end of term finals. I came up with a creative excuse for my teacher, said I'd been sick with a stomach bug. Otherwise, I would be in big trouble with my parents. Jack thought the whole thing was just hilarious since he had no such concerns.

~

Despite that crazy night, I brought Jack home to meet my parents. They liked him. Mum found him humorous because of his crazy ways.

Just months into our relationship, over a candlelit dinner on Valentine's Day, Jack stunned me.

"Will you marry me?" he asked, on bended knee.

My face was aflame, heat rising from my cheeks as strangers' eyes pried into our moment, awaiting an answer.

"Yes," I stammered.

I hardly knew him and said "yes" for all the wrong reasons. I didn't want to ruin the night and disappoint the onlookers, who roared with excitement. Everyone adores a love story with a happy ending.

Jack didn't even have a ring; he was so unprepared. It was nothing like the proposal scenes in the movies. It was a huge let-down. A little voice in my head whispered, "Jack is not Mr. Right," but I ignored it. Perhaps I just wanted to live the fairy tale for a while.

A few days later, Jack took me shopping for my ring at a local jewelry store. I chose an emerald and diamond cluster. Jack smiled and nodded his approval.

In retrospect, it was wrong of me to say yes. But I rationalized my decision: Jack was adopted after his mum had left him at an orphanage; he wanted a new life with the right wife and the right family.

The more I tried to make things work, the more convinced I became that he was not the man of my dreams. Quite the reverse: he started to take advantage of me—staying over in my halls and expecting me to buy the food and cook for him every night. I felt like his mum. Despite the signals, I remained in the relationship far beyond logic.

Weeks later, matters went from bad to worse, as Jack's true colors were revealed. I had introduced my friend Mary's boyfriend, Paul, to Jack. Somehow, the slick-talking Jack managed to borrow £300 from Paul to buy a stupid, big-kid, remote-control car.

Jack was supposedly going to repay Paul out of his work earnings. Nothing happened for weeks, so Paul asked when he would start to see his money. Jack laughed and flat-out refused to repay him.

I felt guilt-ridden about the terrible turn of events since I was the reason Paul had lost a considerable sum of money. "You're such a jerk, Jack, you should pay your debts! You've put me in an awkward, embarrassing position." He just laughed in my face.

I was now certain. I had made another "man-mistake." It was also starting to occur to me; why did I have so much trouble picking Mr. Right? Did I own an aberrant DNA gene? Did I have a broken boyfriend sensor? So, once again, ending the relationship fell on my fragile, increasingly insecure, shoulders.

"I'm sorry, Jack, it's over. You cannot treat my friends like that."

Jack neither protested nor even asked for the ring back.

When I told Mum and Dad what had happened, they weren't even surprised. Mum just said, "Another man with a broken heart." Then we struck a deal. I swapped Jack's emerald and diamond ring with Mum for a pair of new boots. Funny thing, Mum still wears the ring to this day!

~

I rationalized Bad Jack; he was merely another bad choice. I kept telling myself I would know when the right man came along. I was too young to concern myself about such matters. This was my time to be carefree.

In other words, I lied to myself. Again.

8.

A BLACK WIDOW

"Cry. Forgive. Learn. Move on. Let your tears water the seeds of your future happiness."

— Steve Maraboli

2001…

I wondered—despite my wholesome, girl-next-door appearance, was I a Black Widow in disguise?

Someone who easily attracts the opposite sex, sucks the life out of them, and then ends up alone, miserable, and vicious? Or was I just normal and the God of Karma getting her pound of flesh for breaking Will's and Jack's heart?

While I pondered my increasingly screwed-up romances, the university holidays got underway. I needed money to live and socialize until I found Mr. Right to live happily ever after. I began working as a newspaper canvasser, selling papers door to door with my uncle, Mum's brother.

The job took me across the UK, and as the only girl on the team, I was grossly outnumbered, trying to fit into a lad's world (male environment). That's how I met Tim. He was a Londoner, with a strong cockney accent, who shared my love for garage music.

It was two workers per room. So, after spending all day together knocking on doors, we were alone as roommates.

"I'll give you a massage," Tim offered with a devilish smile.

My answer surprised me. "Sure, why not?"

As it turned out, he was an excellent masseur. We did share our first kiss that night and decided we would date.

~

Visiting Tim's mum in North London was an eye-opener. I caught the train to the Big Smoke (London) and experienced my first solo go on the chaotic Tube. It was exciting; I was spreading my wings.

I was not from a super-rich background, but boy, our lifestyles were worlds apart. The stairwell to his mum's flat was covered in graffiti and the stank of urine, but I didn't let on. Tim's mum tried to make me feel welcome; she was a good soul.

Tim changed shirts. I knew he was a bit rough and ready but was shocked to see machete scars on his body. He said they were sustained in a gang attack in his own home. That frightened me a little. "I was taken by surprise," Tim said, "it won't happen again." Tim never told me the full story. And, I didn't press for any details.

I'd lived a sheltered, innocent life in comparison to Tim. Despite my dalliances, I still thought of myself as a naive country girl from a lovely home. Where I came from boys rode bikes, puffed on cigarettes, and had the odd punch up or scuffle, they were certainly not attacked with machetes!

Despite our obvious differences, dating a bad boy like Tim had a certain allure. I was convinced every girl, at one point or another wants to feel the buzz and excitement of being with someone a bit naughty. You know, the type of a boy who is spontaneous, a bit dangerous, and lives life on the edge.

~

Tim claimed he attracted spirits. At first, I thought it was nonsense, until one night in his London bedroom. We were lying in bed; he said, "Do you see it?" I looked up and there was a ball of light floating across the dark ceiling. I trembled with fear. He held my hand. "Don't be afraid; it happens to me all the time," he whispered. "It's probably my dad."

The edges of the orb changed form. It came closer, too close. I couldn't breathe. I was rigid and too scared to take a breath. Tim became afraid too, sensed it was a bad spirit, and started waving his arms and yelling, "Get out! Getaway!"

It was petrifying. I hid under the quilt like a child until it was gone. I'd never experienced anything like it.

Months later, we were still dating when the second paranormal experience occurred. Tim and I were staying in a hotel room above an old pub in Leicester. Another orb starting floating around the room. Unlike the first orb, this one made no sudden advances. Eventually, the ball of light floated to the window, then disappeared. The experience was odd, but I wasn't frightened. Despite Tim's paranormal proclivities, we remained a couple for quite some time.

~

Unlike my other boyfriends, Mum and Dad didn't approve of Tim. They believed he was no good for me and ordered me to end it. I didn't.

The problem is, as a youngster, you defy your parents because you do not like being told what to do. I should have listened.

As time went on, Tim became controlling. I decided to drive home and surprise my family. Tim was heading back from Leicester and staying in Weston with the team. He demanded to see me, but I just wanted to chill with my family after a long drive. He went mad, ringing over and over on route and shouting down the phone.

That distraction led to me smashing into a car in front of me on the motorway. I was blue-lighted to a hospital in West Berkshire and put in a neck brace for whiplash injury. My first car, a little Vauxhall Nova, was written off, and Mum and Dad drove across the country to collect me.

Stupidly, I caved in and visited Tim in my neck brace as I wanted a quiet life and no further arguments. Mum and Dad were unhappy with my decision. Don't ask me why, I do not know myself, but I stupidly stayed in the relationship.

On New Year's Eve, Tim resolved to stop smoking and gave me the last of his cigarettes while partying at a North London pub.

Hours later, walking home with just the moon illuminating our path, Tim grabbed my arm. "Give me my cigarettes!" "No. Don't be silly; you can't break your resolution already!" "Hand them over, now!" "No." That's when he lost it and threw me into a wall. My back smashed into the bricks. I was too stunned to speak and handed them over. We walked on in silence.

I had never encountered his violent physical temper before, only his unkind words leading up to the crash. I became fearful he had a violent side he inherited from his father.

It was the early hours of New Year's Day. We were on the streets in the middle of London. I was scared but had nowhere to go. We went back to his mum's flat, and he started trashing his room, throwing glasses at the wall. His mum calmed him down. I wondered if she was used to such outbursts. It terrified me.

I'd never felt so afraid in a relationship. I'd never experienced any domestic violence in my lifetime. Tim was nothing like kind protective Will. Looking back, I wonder if the orb was a spirit trying to offer me a warning and protection from Tim.

This incident showed me that *the people we think we love, could hurt us*. It also taught me that I should be on my guard and not be so trusting in the future. I would have to be more careful choosing a partner. Of course, as you'll later discover, I was good at making mistakes that would eventually cost me dearly.

Tim was furious when I broke up with him. He stalked me for months, prank called me and hacked into my voicemail.

You are probably asking yourself if I told Mum and Dad what happened to their little girl. The answer is no—I didn't want a lecture; after all, I was a responsible adult at the age of 21.

Enough was enough. I called Tim's mum; told her he'd been harassing me. She was upset. "Vicki, Tim loves you. He's bought an engagement ring and was going to propose to you!"

I replied, "Tell him to go get a refund."

9.

PRINCE CHARMING

"Don't rush into love because even in fairy tales, the happy ending always happens on the last page."

— Anonymous

2001…

By the age of 21, I had already experienced three doomed relationships filled with heartache and pain. I kept telling myself my luck had to change.

Life's storms and missteps had made me impatient; I craved to be loved with no reservations and no judgments by someone who always had my back.

Enter Prince Charming.

~

It wasn't love at first sight with John. But there was an innocence about him. He was more refined, much more of a gentleman than the immature, bad lads I'd dated. I saw his smile, and I knew I wanted to get to know him more. I felt butterflies when we met, he was utterly charming, taking me under his wing to show me the ropes in my new job.

John was my supervisor at Southampton Football Club, and I saw something different in him; genuine kindness. He also danced up a storm behind the bar, exposing his fun side. He was meant to be my superior and oversaw corporate hospitality on match days. I was a barmaid in the supporters' club downstairs.

After a few shifts, John asked: "Fancy a 'lock-in?" The rest is history. We had that drink as promised and a cheeky kiss as he pulled me onto his lap.

~

I'd been asked out on a date by Chris Martsden, a professional Southampton football player, and turned down advances from popstar Pete Devereaux, of Garage sensation, Artful Dodger.

I wasn't interested, despite their fame. I wanted to find myself a true, honest gentleman, and I did, in John. I adored his smile, Irish blue eyes, and quirky dance moves. His sultry voice sealed the deal. At last, I'd found my soulmate.

We'd dated for a week when John whispered those magical three words, "I love you" in Kelly's karaoke bar.

I smiled and answered, "I love you, too."

It sounds crazy, but there was something extraordinary between us. My life as a misguided, young woman was over!

John grabbed the microphone and sang Ronan Keating's *When You Say Nothing at All.* It melted my heart. I'd never been serenaded.

Karaoke was his fun side. It became our song. In time, John added to his song-list Elton John's, *Your Song,* Santana's, *Smooth,* and Right Said Fred's, *Deeply Dippy.* I'll cherish those memories forever.

~

Our relationship moved fast. John sent me love letters via email when I went home for the summer. I still have them 17 years later.

In the letters, he said, "I'll always love you and promise never to let you down." Reading his words made me feel like Her Majesty the Queen. I was head over heels in love. When he closed one letter with, "I have never wanted to say I love you to someone so soon." I was simply breathless.

John kept hinting at a surprise at the end of the month, saying he missed me, loved every minute with me, and that would never change.

The surprise came. Our first weekend break in Hampshire—the 5-star plush, McDonald Botley Grange Hotel. Pretty posh for students!

Something seemed off. John was fidgety, pacing the room. I assumed it was nerves, we had been together three months, but this was our first stay away. John sat on the edge of the bed and plucked a ring box from his pocket. "Will you marry me?" he asked nervously. I was stunned and ecstatic. "Yes," I replied, beaming, my heart on the verge of explosion.

The three-stone diamond trilogy ring was beautiful if a little large. I wrapped toilet paper around it and wore it to dinner, feeling like the luckiest girl in the world.

John said he wanted to share his life with me. I wanted the same; we were magic. I'd finally met my match.

There were only two issues; John hadn't asked my father's permission, and he didn't get down on one knee. I decided to overlook such archaic traditions, but both sets of parents felt the proposal was too soon. After all, we had only been together for three months!

Mum and Dad expressed their concerns. "You'll ruin your degrees." Their comments were upsetting. I explained firmly, "There is no way we will quit university!"

Once we had all met, their skepticism turned to acceptance. We proved everyone wrong and completed our degrees. It was now clear to everyone we were love's young dream. John graduated first and stayed in Southampton while I completed my final year. During that time, we became the envy of every couple. Friends nicknamed us "Posh & Becks." (celebrity couple Victoria and David Beckham). We became the university's poster children for the perfect love.

~

After graduation, we experienced our first challenge. Finding a reporter's job proved trickier than I imagined. It seemed as though every journalism graduate was applying for the declining number of reporting jobs around the country.

John couldn't help but notice I was applying for roles all over the UK. He was angry. "How come we didn't discuss possible locations before you started your mass solicitation?"

I told him, "I didn't see the point until I was offered a real interview."

He misunderstood my response. He thought I would accept whatever job I could find and expect him to follow me like a good puppy dog. That was never the case.

"You can't just expect me to follow you wherever you want! I have a career too," he said.

"You said you hated your career and wanted out of the NHS," I replied," rather harshly.

"I'm just looking at all my options," John said, "don't you trust me?"

I wasn't sure how to answer. I said nothing. That said it all to John. He believed I was determined to have a career of my own —on my terms, and that his job would always come second. That was not true, but it freaked him out.

He decided to dump me. "I love you, but I'm not prepared to move anywhere you want so that *you* can get a job *you* want." I tried to provide a proper explanation—reporting jobs were scarce, trainee ones even rarer. He was not interested in my rationale. He left abruptly, and just ignored all my calls.

Ironically, if I'd been offered an interview somewhere that John did not wish to reside, I wouldn't have gone. I loved him. He was my future and I loved him with every inch of my heart. His rejection put me in an emotional quandary. I cried until no more tears could flow. I did a Bridget Jones—drank wine to excess in the dark and played our favorite love songs in the voicemails I left for John.

Utterly heartbroken and intoxicated, I dragged my tipsy feet through puddles toward the train station. I boarded a train with underwear and socks shoved in a bag and ran home. Mum tried to comfort me. She told me, "Everything is going to be okay." I could see the lie in her eyes; she knew her daughter was broken.

~

I could not imagine life without John.

I needed answers for why my wonderful life seemed always to collapse. Perhaps this was my punishment for breaking boys' hearts in the past?

I set out to find, Madam Tamar, the spiritualist medium who had seen Mum 30 years earlier. Mum told me Madam T had predicted she would marry a man in uniform, move to a sunny country and have a baby. As if by magic, Mum went on a date with an RAF officer. They married, moved to Cyprus, and had my sister Shelly. Surely Madam T could tell me if my future was brighter than my present.

I tracked Madam Tamar down and visited without an appointment. Shivering in the cold drizzle on her doorstep, I was greeted by cats and a little old lady, who looked irate.

She looked into my woeful, sad eyes, and softened as I explained I wanted a reading. "Okay, come in dear out of the rain." She sensed my sadness and sheer desperation.

I had removed my ring to put her to the test. She gave two names; Mary and my ex, Will. "He's still in love with you!"

Next, she told me I was upset over a relationship but promised me it wasn't over.

"He will be back. The number nine is significant."

"It could be nine days, nine weeks, nine months, my dear, but he will be back," she assured. Her prediction gave me goosebumps. Would I wait for nine months? I wasn't sure. All I knew was that I was heartbroken and didn't want to feel this way anymore.

I kid you not; my mobile rang at 9 pm that same night. It was John.

"I'm sorry for the way I acted. It wasn't fair. I love you. Can we try again?"

John wanted me back. He said he realized he'd been foolish, misunderstood my intentions to pick up sticks and leave. I assured him before we would ever pick up sticks and move to a new town, we would make such an important decision together.

~

From that moment on, we were solid, and I was true to my word. So, when a journalist's job I wanted back in my hometown became available, we discussed the opportunity at length. John was happy to come with me and got a job in nearby Cheltenham, working as an accountant for Kraft Foods.

Mum and Dad put us up for a while, in separate bedrooms. Looking back, I loved the fact they were so old fashioned. But we needed our place and soon rented a tiny one-bed house with a lovely spiral staircase. Our landlord seemed okay, though I learned 17 years on, he was the devil in disguise.

10.
ADIDAS MAN

"I can't always be Lois Lane. I want to be superman too."
— Stephanie Meyer

2002…

For as long as I can remember, I wanted to be a high-profile news reporter, pounding the streets chasing bizarre, unexpected stories.

My first role model was Superman's aspirational squeeze, the reporter Lois Lane. Why not? Lois was intelligent, glamorous, loved by everyone, and owned an array of killer heels, like me.

I was now older, and a bit more mature, having graduated with honours in journalism. My role model became Jill Dando, the popular British reporter, who started her newspaper career in my hometown before achieving national stardom. But Jill, the golden girl of British TV, was fatally shot in the head on her Fulham doorstop on 26 April 1999.

The hunt for her killer became the biggest murder inquiry conducted by the Metropolitan Police and the largest criminal investigation since the hunt for the Yorkshire Ripper. A local man, Barry George, was convicted and sentenced to life imprisonment. He was acquitted after a retrial, and Jill's death remains unsolved to this day.

Despite Jill's tragic demise, I still wanted to be the next Jill from Weston. Fate stepped in. After a series of interviews, I was appointed a cub reporter on the *Weston & Worle News,* the main rival to Jill Dando's *Weston Mercury*.

As a newbie, I had a burning desire to be the best, but working in a bustling newsroom was terrifying at the outset. Little did I know I had entered a bitchy, cutthroat business;

everyone vied for the best scoop at the expense of all else. It was my first real-world encounter with the mantra "kill or be killed."

~

As I learned my craft, I became fascinated by the broken criminal minds that took violent liberties with other human beings.

Like magic, along came *Adidas Man*, my shot at instant Dando level stardom. Not quite a serial killer, *Adidas Man* was a vicious serial sex attacker who had darkened our tranquil shore, attacking lone women. For nearly two weeks in September 2002, quaint Weston became a town gripped by fear. Women were too scared to walk the streets. The attacker went on a rampage, struck six women in 13 days. It became one of the biggest manhunts in the history of our seaside town.

What started as a single attack on one 17-year-old girl became an intensive national police search for a mass sex attacker. I was proud to be at the center of the investigation, reporting and keeping everyone updated on the violent activities and the police's intense pursuit of *Adidas Man* in a series of frontpage stories and self-styled bulletins:

- Sunday, September 14, 12.30 am. 17-year-old woman subjected to serious sexual assault on Summerlands Road, in the Earlham Grove area, a mile from the seafront.
- Monday 15, 10.40 pm. 42-year-old woman sexually assaulted by a man on a mountain bike on a path in the Bournville estate, a mile south of the first attack.
- Wednesday 17, 1 pm. 22-year-old approached on the same path by a man on a bike who punches her in the face.
- Thursday 18, 9.30 pm. 18-year-old indecently assaulted on Bournville estate. The description matches two previous attacks on the estate.

- Sunday 21, 3.30 am. 17-year-old attacked near the scene of the first incident.
- Friday 26, 10.30 pm. 42-year-old woman indecently assaulted on a cycle path in Milton Road area, near Earlham Grove. She activates personal alarm, and attacker flees.

The man's modus operandi appeared to be to approach his victim from behind, spin her around, and sexually assault and beat her. Police took the unprecedented step of handing out more than 20,000 rape alarms and warned women not to walk alone. A photofit was issued. The attacker was dubbed 'Adidas Man' due to the Adidas cap and T-shirt he wore during the attacks. He was about 20, six feet tall, with short blond or bleached hair, a long ponytail, and a pierced eyebrow.

~

Things like *Adidas Man* didn't happen in Weston; the town was gripped in fear. It was scary being embroiled in my first major criminal investigation, but it also gave me a vicarious thrill. Identifying *Adidas Man* was my chance to shine. I didn't care if I put myself in danger. I'd pound the streets alone with my pen and pad to get the headlines and by-line. National news and TV crews descended upon our sleepy Somerset town like locusts.

I became bloodthirsty. I was now in competition against the top dogs of Fleet Street. I needed to get the latest scoop and was willing to go to any lengths. Fear was not an option. It was all about being the next Jill. I put on my best suit and heels and began my search for clues at the site of the first attack, the now notorious Bournville estate.

John worried about me and my job. "Be careful out on the estate, don't venture around there alone," he warned. Brazenly, I responded, "I'll be fine. I'm a big girl." He remained silent and supportive; he knew I adored my career.

Numerous press conferences were held, everyone desperate to know if the police were any closer to catching the attacker. They weren't, despite their catchphrase, "We've left no stone unturned."

Officers followed up 1,600 lines of inquiry, checked 450 names, made seven arrests, and held three formal identification parades. But the culprit was never caught. I retraced several of *Adidas Man's* steps, naively thinking I might find a missing detail. I didn't. Suddenly, the attacks stopped. *Adidas Man* vanished without a trace. Like the Fanko (prominent Brazilian politician) assignation, the case has remained unsolved to this day.

Detectives suggested the culprit may have been a holidaymaker who moved on. But his knowledge of paths and cycleways indicated firm local links. All kinds of theories roamed my mind. One thing I did know; *Adidas Man* embedded in me, a passion for crime. Not committing it, of course, but writing about it!

11.

INDECENT PROPOSAL

"A successful marriage involves falling in love many times, always with the same person."
– Mignon McLaughlin

2003…

My ex-boyfriend Will almost ruined my wedding day.

John and I were just about to begin our life together. We had been blissfully in love for two years, and we both had careers we loved. He was a managerial executive with an international spirits company, and I was a reporter assigned to the most controversial stories. I had built a reputation for asking the tough questions and being a relentless guardian of the truth.

I wanted the traditional fairy-tale princess wedding, as did John with all our family and friends present to witness our vows. The "Big Day" was August 2, 2003. We planned a glamorous affair for 100 guests at Batch Country House with its stunning landscaped gardens, a fountain, and a bridge over the lake. It was perfect, as was my sweetheart lace Morilee dress with pearls, crystal beaded embroidery, diamantes, and a gigantic train.

~

Organizing the wedding was fun, but stressful due to some large and small glitches. The trouble began with our wedding party. I had five bridesmaids; my friends Mary, Katherine, Claire, plus my sister Shelley, and John's sister, Cara. They would wear cornflower blue dresses with pearl and diamante beads. Then, out of the blue, the bridesmaid shop went bust and closed without notice.

Fortunately, after I acted like a crazed person, the owner did agree to honor my order and promised to deliver the dresses as contracted. But she lied; I was presented with cheap copies.

"These are imitation dresses; you can still see the dressmakers' chalk on the satin!" I screeched. "I want my money back." I guess my ire scared the devil out of the red-faced owner; she issued a full refund.

With just a couple of weeks until getting hitched, I scoured the surrounding towns to find another bridal store. As things turned out, the gowns were even better, and they cost a bit less!

Next problem, the makeup artist decided to cancel without an explanation, which led to another last-minute save by yours truly. As the hiccups continued, and the August sunshine turned to vicious downpour, every day leading up to the wedding, my stress level rose. In the end, I calmed myself with the belief that it was better for things to go wrong before rather than after being married.

~

The eve of the wedding came. I drove into Mum and Dad's road at sunset, and my heart sank. My ex-boyfriend, Will, was talking to my parents on their driveway. I was flabbergasted! What the hell was he doing there? I didn't have a clue. My stomach twitched nervously.

"Will, whatever are you doing here?"

"Just wanted to come and wish you luck," he said, handing me a wedding card.

Mum, who always had a fond spot for Will, interrupted. "What a nice gesture, why not come in for a drink." Mum stared at me, "Isn't it nice of Will to wish you and John well?"

My instincts told me there was more to his surprise visit. Will walked into the lounge and saw my wedding dress on a mannequin. The train filled the entire room. He burst into tears. I was stunned. His tears came from nowhere. I ushered him into the garden so we could talk. It was then he declared his love.

He begged. "Please don't marry John, marry me!"

I was stunned and shocked, but my response was wimpy, not firm. "Will, you're already married!"

"Yeah, I know that, but I've worked out how much it will cost me to divorce my wife, Vicki (same name!) so that I can be with you. I still love you. I've never stopped loving you. You must know that!"

I was speechless. Will had married a girl years earlier with the same name as mine! What was it with all these Vicki's?

My head was spinning as though I were stuck on a merry-go-round. I wanted to cry. And I did. It was all too much. Will would always have a spot in my heart; he was a good guy. But I was certain John was my soulmate.

~

The more Will pleaded, the more I realized the life I'd started to build with John had only just begun. His love letters proclaimed we would be together forever and ever. He called me the most gorgeous girl in the world, said he thought about me all the time, and loved me more every time we spoke. John made my heart swoon even more, when he told me I had no idea of the depth of his love. *"One day, you'll realize I adore everything about you, and that will make me even happier than I am at this moment."* We were soulmates, and I loved him with my entire being. John was my future, not Will. I knew I had to put an end to Will's indecent proposal at that very moment.

"I'm sorry, Will, you'll always have a place in my heart, but I love John." Tears streamed down Will's face. I felt sick, rejecting him all over again.

Will stared expressionless for what seemed like an eternity, then walked out of my life forever. Or, so I thought. I felt like the cruelest person alive. Not only had I broken his heart once, I'd broken it twice over.

~

My wedding day came. I woke to glorious sunshine and couldn't have been happier. For some reason, I decided to check my voicemails before I began to dress and makeup. My stomach flipped. There were three voicemails from Will. I wept as I listened to the sound of his desperate voice.

"It's me again. I love you. Please don't marry John. I'm outside. Please come down and talk to me. I want you to hear me out."

I looked at the time stamp on the messages. Will had been outside my house since 2 am, begging me to talk to him one more time, hoping I'd come around. I felt terrible that he'd been in the dark alone. At the same time, I knew I'd be crazy to call him on the morning of my wedding. I couldn't cope with the upset, the inner turmoil, so I never returned his calls.

~

The frenetic nature of the pre-ceremony activities buried Will's pleadings. There were bridesmaid catastrophes and families coming in and out with buttonholes as I sat calmly being filmed having my hair done. I was focused on *my* day and loved being styled like royalty.

Stepping into the elegant gown was like becoming a real-life princess. The sun shone through the window, and every gem on my dress glistened. With my tiara and wedding veil secured in place and wearing Aunt Sandra's Victorian ruby and pearl ring as my 'old', I smiled at Mum, and she left with the bridesmaids to get to church.

The house fell silent. Dad and I were alone. When he saw me for the very first time, tears rolled down his cheeks. "My darling, you look beautiful."

"Do you like my dress?" I asked, spinning around, feeling on top of the world.

"You look like a princess."

Dad's comments painted an even bigger smile on my face. I felt like a glamorous beauty queen and knew my life was about to change forever.

"Let's get you to the church on time," Dad said, taking me arm in arm. He looked very much the proud father, as we stepped outside to a smiling welcome committee of our closest neighbors.

I felt like Princess Diana. All eyes cast on me. Today would be the best day of my life. We climbed into the vintage maroon Rolls Royce. My train was so huge, we barely fit. I didn't feel any nerves, just pure excitement that I was going to marry the man of my dreams.

~

The sun was shining, and it was 30 degrees. Every day in the run-up to the wedding had poured with rain. They say the sun always shines on the right people.

"You look so happy, darling, are you nervous?"

"No, not at all. I feel ready, Dad. I love John very much." I was just 22-years-old, but I felt more than ready to become an adult, declare my undying love and marry the man of my dreams.

Dad smiled and gently took my hand. As we reached the church and I stepped out of the Rolls Royce with the sun on my radiant cheeks, my stomach somersaulted. Would Will have the audacity to make another uninvited appearance? I quickly glanced around; there was no sign of him. I painted on a smile to hide my nerves as the photos were taken outside the church. Once inside the church archway, I waited for the wedding procession to begin with a big broad grin on my face.

My mind wandered. I felt a pit in my stomach. Was Will already inside the church waiting to ruin the most important day of my life?

~

Seeing John smiling at the end of the altar, put my mind at ease. The emotion was like nothing I'd ever felt. I was the princess marrying the handsome prince who would adore me forever. The long trail of my dress glided smoothly as Dad proudly walked me down the aisle. The smile on friends, relatives, and especially Mum and Gramps faces made my heart melt. This was John's and my magic moment.

When I arrived at John's side, he smiled, and his eyes glistened. I'd finally found my soulmate to share my life with forever and ever. We exchanged vows, I muddled some words, "I promise to love you until death do us part."

I froze when the vicar asked, "If any person present knows of any lawful impediment to this marriage, he or she should declare it now." If Will was there, there was no legal reason he could give to prevent me from marrying John. Silence lingered in the church for what seemed like an eternity. John smiled at me. We were in the clear! Before I knew it, the vicar announced those special words, "You may kiss the bride." John's lips touched mine for the first time as husband and wife to roars and cheers. I was now a wife after all the heartache.

12.

SUPER MUM

"There will be so many times when you feel you've
failed. But in the eyes, heart, and mind of your child, you
are super Mum."

– Stephanie Precourt

2004…

A flourishing personal career, a smart husband with an international business career, and a loving, close family. I had it all.

While family meant everything to John and me, we agreed to enjoy life as a twosome and build our careers before beginning our family.

The first two years of our marriage were amazing: fun European holidays, buying our first home, and expanding our family with two kittens, Sophie and Alfie.

My career dreams had also come true. I'd swapped from a weekly newspaper to the *Bristol Post*, working as a daily regional reporter. Daily reporters were far more respected than weekly journalists. I'd make a name for myself.

As John climbed the corporate ladder, his job frequently started taking him abroad, away from home. I was often left alone while he ventured to Europe to visit other offices in Copenhagen and Porto, Portugal. These visits were for business meetings, and I had to put up with it.

~

We'd only been married for six months when, for the first time, I started to feel lonely, perhaps taken too much for granted. I hated being in the house with just two kittens for company. I was convinced John was trying to excel in his career to improve our quality of life, but I missed him being by my side every day.

Mum and I traveled on a girls' break to the Algarve. It was during this trip, that I decided it was time to have a family, even though I was only 24. John had already lost two grandparents, and his grandfather was now ill. Gramps was also unwell at the time, and I wanted my grandparents to see our children.

"Let's start a family," I suggested.

"Okay," said John, welcoming the idea. We both felt it would strengthen our marriage bonds. I fell pregnant straight away and discovered I was having a healthy baby boy.

During my pregnancy, I continued to stomp the streets chasing crime stories, pretending I was Lois Lane.

It still gave me a rush, and I loved the thrill of seeing my scoops on the front page. Even the nationals followed my lead—printing two of my high-profile scandals—"Copping Off" and "The Dogging Copper."

"Copping Off" exposed a policeman caught having sex at the police station, and "The Dogging Copper" uncovered a carpark tryst with an on-duty officer and a married couple.

The uniformed officers' pictures were plastered across front pages. I felt guilty for telling the whole world, but their careers were already over; their fate sealed by their actions. I merely exposed the reason for their suspension.

"Copping Off" was shortlisted for *The Press Gazette* national award, a momentous achievement. I understood that the story went far deeper than I could publicly divulge. Had I shared key details about the women involved, you'd understand why there was no hesitancy on my part in printing it. That, however, is a secret I'll take to my grave to protect them.

One of the many lessons I learned during my crime-fighting days was that there were good cops, bad and a few naughty ones who, despite their allegiance to the law, let their own vices cloud their judgment.

~

I worked for as long as I could, right up until almost my due date. Then came a moment that made me realize I was carrying a precious life, and I needed to protect him.

A body had been found in a ditch in upscale Flax Bourton. He was identified as a local Weston man. I did the natural thing and visited his home to speak to his next of kin and to write a tribute story.

It meant door knocking on the notorious Bournville estate, but I needed to learn how the poor man ended up dead in a ditch, some 15 miles away from his home.

Two men in suits approached me on the stairwell, eyed me up and down, flashed police badges. "What's your business here, love?"

"Love"—how condescending!

"I'm a reporter for the Bristol Post. I'm looking for a next of kin to the dead man."

"Take our advice. It's not safe here. Especially, given your condition. We would advise that you leave the premises." My unborn baby was already my most prized possession, and I wasn't about to put him in danger and lose him. I fled quickly.

~

Not long after, I set off on maternity leave. My angel, Matthew, was born on October 4, 2005, weighing 7lbs 10.5 oz.

I'd rushed to Bristol, had been told I had six hours at least, but the eager little monkey shocked everyone—he arrived just 10 minutes later.

That moment, when the midwife placed him in my arms, was like nothing I'd ever felt. I was a mum to a perfect, beautiful boy.

"He's perfect, well-done baby," John whispered.

Seeing my little bundle being cuddled by John, Mum, Dad, Nan, Gramps, and my sister, was a wonderful feeling. I'd brought a new member into the family and felt proud. Matthew became the apple of my eye. He was the first grandchild in our family and was adorable.

He just didn't like sleep and cried relentlessly. Exhausted, I felt like all I did was feed him 24 hours a day. I never envisaged motherhood could be so draining.

John would try to assist by driving down the motorway in the middle of the night. The purr of the engine seemed to soothe Matthew. He'd return, switch off the engine, and the cries would start again. Then I'd cry, frustrated. I was so tired, my eyes stung.

I remember John bringing him to me, saying he must be hungry again. I yelled at him, "I'm not a bloody milking machine!" That always makes me laugh, looking back.

We had it tough for the first month, unlike those annoying mum's who claim their child slept through on Night One. I discovered the solution was pre-made baby formula. Soon, Matthew was a different child and slept.

~

I was a mum and career woman working from home while balancing a family and a traveling husband. The only time my mum status proved difficult was the morning of July 28, 2008; the Grand Pier inferno, a fire which took Britain by storm.

I'd received a text saying the attraction was ablaze at 6 am. I thought it was a joke. But the texts started coming through fast. I rushed out of bed, chucked on some clothes, and called Mum.

"Mum, the pier is on fire! Can you watch Matthew for me?"

"Of course," replied Mum. I took my son to his nan's in his PJs and headed for the shore armed with a pad and pen.

Our iconic town landmark was buckling amid a massive fire, and I was a reporter on the ground, watching the devastation unfold. News spread fast. All eyes around the globe were on our little seaside town and the Grand Pier inferno. I was even reporting to copy takers (newsroom assistants who type up stories over the phone) live from the beach.

It was a great buzz and a story that lasted for weeks. The rebuild coverage lasted even longer; I was writing pier story updates for the next two years. Somehow, during all this activity,

I became a proud mum again. My beautiful daughter, Emily, had entered the world in January 2010, weighing 6 lbs 10.5 oz.

I was truly one goddamn sensational supermum!

13.

PHYSICALLY BROKEN

"Pain doesn't show up in our lives for no reason. It's
a sign that something needs to change."

– Bipasha Barua

2010…

*As a self-proclaimed successful multitasker, I set my sights on
gathering a few prestigious journalism awards to feel self-fulfilled. Fate
thought otherwise.*

The Grand Pier reopened in October 2010 with a double-
page story proclaiming the rides were bigger and better than ever
before. I was a VIP press guest for my coverage of the fire, and
the continued publicity as it underwent restoration. During the
opening day festivities, one of the inventors asked me to take the
first ride in his new ride, The Whip.

I was excited; I was a momentary celebrity. "We'll give you a
good spin," said the operator. I didn't know he'd set the ride
speed to "extreme," which turned out to be a BAD, BAD, BAD
decision. The ride whipped me around like a rubber doll; I could
feel a snap in my back. I held on for dear life, screaming to no
avail. My spine was not strong enough to withstand the intensity
of the ride during the sharp twists and turns. Minutes later, the
whip came to a halt.

"I can't move," I cried to my photographer. I attended
Accident & Emergency immediately at my local hospital. They
were useless. They sent me away, suggesting I take paracetamol
since my injury was probably nothing more than a muscle pull. I
left in sheer agony. Months earlier, the same hospital had sent
John home with snapped cruciate ligaments in his knee, so I had
little faith in them.

~

Life became a struggle. I had the perfect family, perfect job, and a loving husband. I struggled to work despite the never-ending pain and the need to look after our two wonderful children.

The doctors had said taking regular doses of paracetamol should make things right. At first, I followed those instructions, but the pain worsened. John and I chose to pay for a private osteopath. *To hell with socialized medicine!*

It felt as though every appointment was useless, as was the expensive pain relief gel she sold me. The pain was not subsiding; it was worsening with every day, and every step I took. I felt broken.

Having given birth twice with no pain relief, I could not understand why I was in so much constant agony but continued to get from day to day, playing Lois Lane and mum.

~

While I was recuperating, a surreal incident happened that changed my outlook on the world of reporting.

A close contact, a local married businessman named Terry, who owned a popular bar called Seven, was accused of beating his girlfriend. I was shocked that he could be accused of such behavior. I was even more shocked when my editor asked me to attend the court case and write the story. He had no idea I knew Terry. I tried to explain that he was a close contact of mine and had provided me with many 'tip-offs' over the years. That didn't make a difference. "It's frontpage material. A story's a story," he said. "And, this one seems to have an odd twist." He paused, "Isn't that your specialty?"

When I arrived at court, our eyes met. He begged me, "Vicki, don't cover my case, please. We go back years; you know the real me."

I was professionally conflicted. I thought about how Jill Dando would have handled the situation. The answer was clear.

"Terry, I'm sorry, but the head office sent me here. I can't turn a blind eye." He rolled his eyes like a wounded puppy, then angrily stomped away. I could see he was a man who didn't like it when he didn't get his way. I saw a side of Terry that said he *could* have beaten his girlfriend in anger.

Nevertheless, had HQ not sent me, and no other reporters had been present, I might have honored Terry's demand. But as the proceeding continued, the CCTV footage was undeniable. Terry was quickly found guilty. I felt vindicated.

~

Weeks later, I ended up with a few friends in Terry's bar to celebrate a birthday. Drunk, and at rock bottom, he became abusive, shoved me, and started to shout, "Get out of my fucking club, bitch." Having witnessed the court assault footage, I started to back up. My horrified friends stood by my side, and we left.

When we got home, John and I talked. He raised a very real issue, "Isn't your safety more important than writing stories?'

I thought about it for a few moments. John was right. I had already been given the go-ahead by my news editor, Ron, to do non-competitive public relations work on my own time. So my next professional step seemed logical. In time, I'd quit journalism and set up my own PR firm.

Unfortunately, somebody in the newsroom hierarchy disagreed with Ron's decision. Next thing I know, he embarrassed me in public view, "I never gave you permission to do private PR. That's a terrible example for the staff. You are facing a disciplinary (a meeting between an employer and an employee to discuss an allegation of gross misconduct)! I was stunned and upset by his betrayal. I would never have undertaken private PR work; had I not been granted permission!

As if Ron's public berating was not enough, my back pain had worsened. I cried after I dropped Matthew at school, taking pathetic steps back to my car like an old woman with my wooden cane.

Dealing with two major battles at once does try even the most determined soul like me! My career was in shambles, and my body was wracked with pain.

I managed to drive after demanding an urgent appointment with my osteopath. She could see that I was declining fast when I hobbled through the door. With minutes, she confirmed my entire world was caving in around me!

"I'm sorry to say this, Vicki, but your back is not responding as I hoped it would. Looking at your current state, I fear the worst." She paused and stared at me for what felt like an eternity.

"What does 'the worst' mean?" I blurted.

"I'm afraid that you may have a slipped disc, and it's pressing on the nerves, which is why you are now having trouble walking. If you don't get seen by a surgeon soon, you could lose the feeling in your legs." I was stunned.

John's work insurance provided urgent private medical care. I was seen by a top back specialist at the prestigious Spire Bristol Hospital. The x-rays and MRI scans were definitive: I had two slipped discs and a foreboding prognosis. "You need major spinal fusion surgery."

The specialist added that my discs resembled cat food. "It's the worst case I've ever seen. How you've been walking around is beyond me. You must have a very high pain threshold."

"Are there surgical risks?" I asked. I could barely take in his words.

"Mrs. FitzGerald, there are risks associated with any major surgery: nerve damage, scar tissue, infection, heart attack, and stroke."

Jesus, I smiled. "Anything else?"

He hesitated, "There's a very small chance you might not survive, but that risk is so minuscule, I wouldn't worry about it."

Don't worry about it, I thought! I was frightened out of my mind.

I choose to dawdle a bit longer, having been given Cortisone (steroid) injections first. "The Cortisone should help with pain and inflammation, but your case is so severe, I doubt it will have any effect." I'd take anything. I just wanted to pain to stop and life to be normal again if it were remotely possible.

14.

CRACKS IN THE MIRROR

"There is a crack in everything. That's how the light gets in, sometimes."

— Leonard Cohen

2010…

Sometimes, as we battle through life's challenges, cracks grow, and some become unfixable.

My little bundle of joy, Emily, was born in January 2010— just three days before my beloved Gramps was diagnosed with a terminal illness.

I was beyond devastated. My hero, the man I had looked up to since I was a kid, had been given a short timestamp. Despite the hand he had been dealt, Gramps remained jovial and upbeat, determined to prolong his life by undergoing treatment. He wanted to see his great-grandchildren grow up. Watching a strong-willed gentleman wither and lose strength was unbearable. It all seemed so unfair.

Despite my outwardly cheery appearance, I was angry and bitter inside. Why Gramps? What had he ever done to anyone? Was there a God? And, if there was, what the hell was he thinking?

~

Just when I thought life couldn't get any worse, it did! Two weeks after Gramps Albert died, my other Grandad, Jack, died. Saying goodbye to the dual heartbeats of our family was the worst moment of my life. My perfect little life with my perfect husband, perfect kids, and perfect family spiraled out of control.

My grief was overwhelming, and every day seemed like a battle for survival. My disc pain only heightened the grief. In the process, I discovered that when you lose someone you love without reservation, there will forever be a vital piece missing somewhere deep inside. Life can be lived, but it never is the same again.

Why am I telling you this? Hopefully, so you can avoid some of the bad choices I've made. When you hit the inevitable bumps in the road of life, you need to understand how to tackle enemy #1—Grief. Grief has the power to grip your soul and infest your mind.

I let all that happen and more. I never recovered. I graduated from pain and loss to depression. Maybe that's why I made so many bad choices.

~

Gramps taught me never to quit. So, despite my ordeals, I vowed to fix me, physically and mentally. I had to, for my kids and my sanity.

A month after the death of my grandfathers, I was admitted for the surgery, ignoring the complication warnings. I had no choice. I couldn't go on as I was. I wanted my parents, husband, and my children to love the woman they used to know.

The doctor explained while I was on the gurney not far from the operating theatre, "The surgery should repair the disc pressing on the nerves." Since I was heavily sedated, I remembered him saying something about the second disc remaining broken, and they would probably require the need to cut my entire back open. I remembered thinking, "Jesus f… Christ."

My last image was John, acting assured and cheery, "You'll be fine, it will be over in no time," he assured as I closed my eyes, falling under sedation, and was wheeled into theatre.

The operation lasted five hours but was a success. I came around feeling high and told my surgeon, "You could have given me a boob job while you were there!" (I had always thought I was short-changed when it came to boobs!). To John, the return of my sense of humor meant he still saw the woman he married, despite all the little challenges. Thankfully, there were no complications, other than a minor post-op infection. With the help of physical therapy and family support, I was walking "relatively" normally in six weeks.

But as I was to learn, there would be a lot more shit rolling downhill. During my recuperation, another blow arrived. Sally, my son's kind, sweet childminder, dropped dead while walking along the street. She was 41. Sally's heart stopped for 15 minutes before paramedics revived her. Her brain was starved of oxygen, causing a severe brain injury.

"She's on ITU. I warn you, seeing her is very distressing," her husband warned. I didn't care. Sally was part of our family, almost. But seeing her was another story. I barely recognized the woman before me and could not hold back my tears. The Sally I knew was long gone. They had even cut off all her wonderful blonde locks into a spiky short cropped style. It was like looking at a stranger.

Amazingly, she battled the odds and learned to walk and talk. I continued to offer my support and visited her in the rehabilitation unit frequently. Sally was left blind, and her speech was impaired. The horrific ordeal only added to my upset with God.

~

Then there was the disciplinary hearing with my employer, the *Post* newspaper while I was trying to recover, care for a child and baby, and be a good wife. I was accused of running my PR company in my spare time without their permission (yet I'd had it in writing from my news editor, Ron). I didn't have the strength to argue my case. I felt ill and exhausted.

A private discussion with my news editor was more of a tribunal than an explanation of my benefits and rights. First, he reprimanded me for setting up a public relations business while in their employment. I explained it was "agreed prior" by him.

He ignored my comment. "What's happened to the Vicki that I knew?" I burst into tears.

"You don't want to know," I said perhaps too flippantly.

He responded, "Try me."

"Truthfully, I can no longer take the bullying from my colleague Heidi. It has been going on for months. She's been desperate to push me out of my job. Even the editor at the *Weston Mercury* met with me and revealed Heidi's intention to give my job to her best friend once I'd been outed! That's the reason I've set up in PR so that I can leave my job for good. I can't take it anymore."

Then my News Editor put a dagger through my fragile heart. "Can't you forget about the bullying? Put it behind you?"

"No," I replied as I handed him a file of all the evidence I'd gathered, the proof of the constant bullying in documented emails.

Next thing I knew, I was offered redundancy (permanent settlement). The *Post* wanted to bury the bullying allegations and avoid me taking them to a tribunal.

That night I sat on the edge of the bed staring at the cracks in the mirror.

John walked in. "What's wrong?"

I sobbed. "I don't know what's happening to me. I'm an emotional wreck; everything has become too much. I want to cry forever."

John didn't know what to do or say. He felt awkward. I wanted him to take me in his arms and tell me that I'd be okay. He didn't. That was the first time during our marriage that he made me feel truly lonely and rejected. I'd wanted his love and support, but I was given neither. It felt as though the chemistry was gone and John did not love me anymore. I was gutted. All I'd needed to stop my tears was a cuddle, but John simply stared as though he no longer recognised me.

Instead, he suggested I visit the GP. I felt even more alone because he didn't know how to handle me. But, then again, neither did I! John didn't even offer to come with me.

Gramps would have known how to fix me; woven my broken seams back together and reignited my lost spark. I longed for him to come back.

15.

LOST IN THE CROWD

**"Depression isn't just being a bit sad. It's feeling nothing.
It's not wanting to be alive anymore."**

— JK Rowling

2014…

*From the outside, I was at the top of my game as the director of
my new firm, Paramount PR. Underneath, it was an entirely different
story.*

My GP listened attentively—her diagnosis: complex depression.

"Vicki," she analysed correctly, "You have a lot on your plate; grief, injury, stress, and physical recuperation, while wanting to be a responsible mum."

Translated—I was lost in the crowd and didn't know how to fix myself. Correction—I didn't know if I could ever fix myself.

"I would consider a little medication," she suggested. "It will help manage your emotions."

"I don't want antidepressants," I retorted. "I'm not crazy."

"I didn't say you were. Millions of people take antidepressants to help them feel like their old selves."

I softened. "What are you suggesting?"

"Citalopram. Just a small 10mg dose. It's safe and mild, used properly."

I decided *what the hell did I have to lose.*

~

Drinking alcohol while taking Citalopram was not advised, but as you've surmised by now, I don't like being told how to live my life. So, when my neighbor, Maria, would come over, most days at 5 pm, let herself into my house with her open bottle of wine, we'd sit and chat till the bottle was empty. She, too, was on antidepressants, had been for decades, and drinking hadn't done her any harm.

Things were changing on the marital front. John's career was flying. He was moving up the corporate ladder and was staying away three times a week in London. I was at home alone with the kids, still recovering, but I felt enormously proud of him for chasing his dreams.

John was working to support our family but was able to enjoy nights out in the city, fine dining, and rubbing shoulders at swanky London venues and celebrity restaurants.

At first, I envied his lifestyle without me. Then I started to wonder, was there something else going on?

We were now living worlds apart. I was stuck home while he was staying in posh London hotels and getting drunk with male and female colleagues. I'd hear giggling girls in the background, and my imagination ran wild.

I decided to do some snooping on his Hotmail, and what I discovered broke my heart—a message from another woman, Michelle, saying, "Great to see you last week. xx"

It was a punch to the stomach. I was at home working and playing mum, cleaning up baby sick, and doing the school runs, and he was out having dinner with another woman!

Sickened, I confronted John. He was angry and said that he had bumped into a university pal in the city. I was such a stupid fool; I took his word because I didn't want to believe he could cheat. If it were innocent, why didn't he tell me about their encounter? Why keep it secret? I let the matter drop, but when he was away, I'd sit and wonder.

At the work summer party, I caught a pretty brunette, Rebecca staring at John and me. I could see the obvious longing in her eyes when she smiled at him. I knew I didn't imagine her interest, as when she spoke to us, there was an obvious awkwardness. I confronted John.

"Why is Rebecca acting so strange?"

"Vicki, you're overreacting."

I knew Rebecca, and two other colleagues, Christina, and Kate stayed over in London regularly. The latter was married, unlike single, shady Rebecca, but I was forced to accept his word, even after another 'off' encounter at Kate's wedding. Maybe I was a fool. I'll never know, and he was never going to admit to adultery.

There were also those nights when he didn't come home from nights out in Bristol. He'd ended up staying in a hotel or on a mate's sofa! I would sit quietly by the fireplace in the early hours of the morning, settling our crying baby and wonder why he wouldn't answer his phone and why he chose not to come home to his loving wife.

Perhaps he couldn't deal with my depression—I wasn't fun to be around anymore. I told myself to get a grip; I loved John so much, I had decided to turn a blind eye. I didn't want to lose him like previous boyfriends I had discarded.

~

Life went on. But we continued to drift further apart. Intimacy became less and less. We needed to rediscover each other again.

Having recovered from my injury, I went flat out, acquiring clients for my new PR company. It grew fast. I wasn't just a mum anymore. My PR was in demand through word of mouth. I felt proud of myself. My days became stressful and crazy: I'd do the school run at 8.45 am, work all day, go to school again, cook, bathe and put the kids to bed, and work again until 11 pm. I was driven by professional pride and insecurity. I needed to succeed. I didn't want to be a failure. I couldn't be. That would set me back into the depression trap.

I gained major tourist attractions, a theatre, six leisure centres, a restaurant chain, plus much more. Little old me—I had become a success. It wasn't huge sums. I was never going to be a highly paid corporate executive like John, that was unrealistic, but I had become a respected local businesswoman. I even came off the antidepressants; I no longer felt sad. Life again had a purpose.

I thought this newfound success would make me more attractive to John, but he never noticed, he was consumed with building his career and achieving his goal of becoming a company director.

~

On those rare days and nights when John wasn't working, his social calendar was full. He'd coach kids' football on Wednesday nights, play adult footie, Thursday, go to premier league matches, and play football tournaments almost every Saturday and Sunday. I felt neglected, and so very, very lonely.

My parents joked, "You're a football widow" because Emily and I attended family BBQs and roast dinners without John and Matthew. Their comments were true and instilled further sadness. Why was football more important?

Work and football took over his life. There was no time for us. It was heart-breaking. I pleaded, "Please, John. Cut the football down. It's ruining our marriage." John brushed my comments off. Perhaps there was more to our failing marriage. I was drowning in a sea of disappointment, without a life preserver to rescue me.

It was clear; we were no longer the keepers of a traditional marriage. On weekends, John focused on being a team boy (dad and son relationship) with him and Matthew. I know he wanted to be a good dad, but I often wondered why being a great dad was more important than being a great husband. Emily was also left out of the equation and longed for daddy-daughter time I became convinced John didn't want to be around me and my growing insecurities. Perhaps I was misguided, but I knew I wasn't the first wife that cried out for affection and respect.

Again, when confronted about why his phone was always on silent and face down, John suggested my imagination was running wild. His solution? Ignore me and continue with his commitments while I become a team girl, spending my weekends with our daughter. While it wasn't the answer I sought, Emily knew being team girl would mean we'd get quality time together. That was important. In many ways, she was all I had. I didn't get to have the same quality time I craved with Matthew—he was always at football. It sounds sad, but I felt as though John was taking my son away from me, ruining our special bond.

~

Socializing with me became equally unsatisfying.

I couldn't recall the last time John and I had been on a date, just the two of us. Instead, we would simply go to the pub with a group of friends and hang out together. I'd be chatting to the girls, and he'd stand at the bar with the men. I wasn't crazy about the gender separation, but nobody else seemed to mind. I rationalized this was the natural order, the longer people were married.

If only Gramps were still alive. He would have told me the secret to how he and Nan kept their magic over all the years.

The sad reality was that HIS focus had become to develop our friendship circle and not our marriage. Maybe John was happy with this new way of life—he got to have a wife and have a bachelor's lifestyle, drinking with the lads. It was far from what I wanted. I needed to feel loved. It's part of my DNA.

As the intimacy of our relationship faded into this adjusted reality, I realized I had become collateral damage. The old fun-loving, self-confident Vicki was gone. I wondered, would it stay that way forever?

At that moment I didn't know the answer.

16.
DIRTY LITTLE SECRETS

"Sweetie, if you are going to be two-faced,
at least make one of them pretty."
— Marilyn Monroe

2014…

Sometimes you dream of a new life, a new home. It doesn't always turn out the way you had anticipated, but that's life!

The more I tried to be a respectful, dutiful wife, the more unnoticed and unloved I felt. It was also terribly clear; I didn't deal with personal stress very well, despite my business successes. I became more withdrawn.

Matthew noticed I wasn't my cheery self. He asked, "Mum, are you alright?" To put his mind at ease, I'd make up excuses like, "Mum's fine, just some problems at work." John also noticed a change in my personality, but he chose not to inquire —even once.

It just seemed as though John and I were purely existing, living two lives; his with Matthew, mine with Emily. I wondered whether our marriage would survive. I also rationalized that no matter what happened between John and me, the children would be the living proof that our marriage had its better moments. I was confident Matthew and Emily loved me without reservation and knew I would protect them no matter what.

~

One summer day, "no matter what" made a surprise appearance.

I heard Matthew screaming in front of our house. The sound was excruciating; my heart raced; my stomach felt gutted.

I ran, as fast as I could, toward his cries and found Matthew clutching hold of his bloody leg, inches from a Staffie (a vicious Staffordshire Bull Terrier) baring its razor teeth. I scooped him into my arms and stared in horror at the blood as tears gushed down his cheeks. His little leg was punctured with bite marks. We rushed him to Accident & Emergency at the hospital. Bruises quickly emerged around each of the wounds, and the doctors could see the outline of the dog's jaw.

John insisted we talk to the owner to get the dog muzzled so that no other child in our street could face potential harm. When confronted, the owner blamed Matthew. "It's your damn kid's fault. He stepped on my lawn, getting his ball. My dog was only protecting what was his."

I was furious. "He's just a seven-year-old boy. Your dog is dangerous and should be muzzled! And, I've heard this isn't just the first time it has attacked someone!"

Despite the fact the dog had attacked before, charges could not be filed because the law, at that time, stated: "an owner could not be prosecuted if someone is attacked on his private property."

The Dangerous Dog Act was amended months later, but Matthew's case could not be reopened. John was furious with the outcome. We feared it could happen again because it was quite normal for kids to play in the cul-de-sac, and the owner continued to tie up both of his Staffie dogs outside his house. We both agreed we no longer felt safe in our neighborhood.

One night we sat silently in the living room—John on his iPad, me on my laptop. "What are you doing?" John asked. "Looking at houses!" I replied.

John smiled. "Me too."

That was it. We decided to leave our long-time neighbors, and move to upscale Wick, make new friends through the kid's school. Why Wick? The houses were larger, more upmarket, and the area was still in walking distance to school. It didn't take long to find a showcase home with a hefty price tag. We decided we could afford it, with John's increased salary and bonuses, and my PR firm's revenue.

My goal was to make-over the show-home so we would become a family again. The place had two annexes: we turned one into a fifth bedroom for guests, and the other into a hot tub room with a bar. I thought it would be a cool place to chitchat with friends over a glass of wine.

When the remodel was complete, I proudly announced, "our hot tub room is open for business." John's response? "Oh." In the ensuing months, not once did he get into the hot tub with me. He just wasn't interested. And when it came to sexual relations, I was the one who continued to make advances, not John. I felt more and more neglected. I'd gone from a bubbly, fun girl to a woeful, sad soul who felt ugly and unloved because John didn't want me.

~

Things quickly went from bad to dreadful! I lost my biggest public relations client while John was traveling on business. My client had burnt through their cash by taking on too many new projects. I was collateral damage in their cost-cutting. They had been my largest retainer; their fees covered much of my overhead. I was now professionally desperate and personally depressed. Bottom line, I was all alone dealing with business issues, no old friends nearby, a disinterested husband, two demanding children, and a new puppy named Bella that needed constant attention. Somehow, I had become the man of the house and had taken a road less traveled without a Plan B.

Fortunately—or so I thought—I made new friends at the children's school, and most of them lived in Wick. I was quickly welcomed into the "School Mummies Circle," where the topics of the day were new restaurants, ugly rumors, and dirty little secrets. I also learned many club members were snorting cocaine and having affairs. I was beyond shocked. I was familiar with social drinking, but cocaine was a whole new world to me. I was asked on more than one occasion if I wanted a toot or two, but I always managed a plausible excuse.

Outings to the local pub with the new friends became the norm. John would try to keep up with the lads. I'd equally match the girls. Our friends became our focus, and not each other—big mistake.

As friendships grew, I discovered more and more of their secrets. Nearly everyone seemed to be "at it;" their familial relationships were just a facade.

One evening, one of my new friends got nosey, "What do you do with your time since your husband travels so much?" I responded obtusely. I thought to myself, why would I cheat on John? I loved him too much, and I remained confident we would solve our difficulties.

I'd even given myself a new make-over with glossy hair extensions and had taken up running. I tried my best to look more attractive to John. I wanted him to love me and look at me the way that he used to, but I was fighting a losing battle. Perhaps seeing your wife experience grief, depression, and walking in pain with a cane, altered his feelings.

The more time we spent with friends and the more secrets I learned, I had a little inkling that some of these new friends would become toxic, alter my outlook about values, and ruin John and me, forever.

~

Eventually, I came to realize that a new start does not fix things. I've often wondered looking back, suppose we had not bought the big house? Suppose we had never met those troubled school friends? If nothing had changed, would John and I have patched things up, and been happier?

The answer? I'll never know. But I did learn, a new start in a big new house doesn't automatically fix things.

I also learned *some of the most poisonous people come disguised as friends.*

I just learned it a little too late.

17.
FATBOY42 & SUNSHINE GIRL

"We are each our own devil.
And, we make this world our own hell."

— Oscar Wilde

2016…

Fate acts in mysterious ways. It often puts you on a new path, only sometimes that re-route can have deadly consequences.

As a journalist, I always felt a good, old-fashioned, heart-pounding rescue at sea made for a great read. Over the years, I'd written many such stories because we lived in coastal communities. That's how I got to know Coastguard, Mark. He had helped me flush out my stories for more than a decade. I considered him a close friend, and our paths crossed almost daily with our dogs and children.

Mark was also the organizer of a multi-terrain running event in Somerset. He wanted this year's race to be a huge fundraising success, so he asked if I would help do some pro bono public relations work. Even though I was stretched to the max with kids and a crumbling marriage, I agreed to help—that's what friends do.

"Vicki," said Lara, "sometimes you are just so naive. He doesn't just want PR help; he wants you. Haven't you noticed the way he looks at you?"

"Nonsense," I retorted. "We're just friends, and he's married!"

"I don't know any married man who just wants to be friends with a married woman," glared Lara. I didn't agree.

~

Christmas arrived. Mark messaged to say his dog had died. He was devasted, as was his family. I felt sorry for him because my dog Bella was part of our family—I could understand his agony.

Mark couldn't cope. He promptly acquired a new puppy and eagerly introduced him to Bella. We walked and regularly talked about nothing in particular. Initially, I was oblivious to his flirting, but I did look forward to our walks. It had become a private time for each of us to offload our problems, and in my eyes, it was friendship, nothing more.

"My wife is awful," said Mark out of the blue. "She doesn't even cook for me!"

"Well, I'm a football widow," I joked. "I rarely have a husband to cook a meal for."

We both laughed. It seemed no one I knew had THE perfect marriage. I figured that's what happened in long term relationships—the buzz and the excitement fades, replaced with daily stresses.

"If you were mine, I'd never do that to you," he said. I took his flirt as a pleasant compliment, nothing more.

We'd walked for another month before Mark upped his flirting to another level. He started complimenting me regularly in short texts on Messenger. "You looked gorgeous today. I enjoyed spending time with you." Then he stunned me, adding, "I've been flirting with you for months, but you've not even noticed."

Those compliments, the way he looked adoringly at me with a glint in his eye, revived my still heart. It was a feeling for which I longed. I just wanted to feel special. Before long, we became messaging machines. It had been a long time since my husband had paid me a compliment that made me feel good about myself, and, after all, John had his 'other' life in London.

"Dogging today?" became our standing catchphrase with regards to walking the dogs. Our conversations became increasingly personal. I knew we were headed for a heap of trouble, but I was envious of the double lives that my friends were leading and knew John had enjoyed dinner (at least) with another woman.

I guess, I just wanted the attention that I richly craved from John and never received. Mark happened to be there, in the right place, at the right time. I should have been stronger, ignored his flattery, but everyone makes mistakes—Mark was mine. Sometimes good people make bad choices. It doesn't mean they are bad; it means they're human.

~

My 35th birthday came. I had lunch with former *Post* colleagues. Mark called to wish me a happy birthday. "Come over to my house on the way to school and let me wish you a proper happy birthday," he flirted.

I was pleasantly horrified.

"Just pop over, and then we can walk to school together," he replied. I didn't see the harm, we pretty much walked to school most days.

As soon as I stepped inside his marital home, I smelled fresh paint from their new extension. He offered a devilish smile. I stood awkwardly as we chatted in his new dining room. There was a glint in his Bombay Sapphire eyes. Suddenly, he pounced on me like a panther!

I hadn't expected it, but equally, I did not stop him. That was very wrong of me and something I will regret to the day I die. That one kiss altered my life, forever. But I stupidly let it happen. I could feel the excitement as he kissed me with wild intensity, and I inhaled the seductive scent of his woody-amber Armani cologne. My pores tingled. We were one. There was no time for guilt.

I'd been neglected and rejected as a woman for so long, made to feel unattractive like an ogre, despite being a sporty size eight and always taking care of my appearance. Mark's chase was refreshing; there was nothing wrong with me after all. I was still attractive to the opposite sex.

My lust intensified, I decided *to hell with the rules*. Most people I knew were at it, including two of my best friends, and I also suspected John of infidelity. Why shouldn't I have some fun too?

I desperately wanted John to love me, had tried so very hard to reignite the spark with romantic dinners, and sexy underwear, but something had changed. His business focus, his constant travel, and his lack of attention made me sad and lonely. Cracks had emerged that couldn't be fixed; the damage was irreversible.

I craved companionship with someone who wanted to spend time with me, show an interest in me as a person and make me feel cherished. Mark did all that and more. He brought me back to life.

I know my promiscuous behavior sounds terrible, it was, and it is extremely regrettable. Remember, once you cross the line, you cannot go back.

~

After our birthday get-together, the nature of our walks changed. There were tender kisses along the way in discreet lanes and nonstop messages. We couldn't go an hour without being in contact and spoke or Facetimed at every opportunity. Often, we'd talk for two hours while he drove home from Maidenhead, but the time flew.

Mark suggested we create private Twitter accounts, so we would not get caught on Messenger. He knew what he was doing. I did wonder if he had done it before, but that was none of my business. He was Fatboy42, and I was SunshineGirl.

Every morning I'd wake to the message: "Morning, gorgeous girl." I felt as though I had a new lease on life.

When Mark worked at home, we'd meet in secret at his home or drive out of town for lunch dates. I feel bad about those encounters, but I rationalized it was his idea, not mine. Originally, I thought to myself, "his choice." As I reflect today, I'm disgusted with myself. I should have had the guts to decline his interest or leave John if I was unhappy. My advice: *be honest about your feelings and be honest with each other. Deceit is the worst feeling in the world.*

~

John noticed a change in my behavior. I had a spring in my step and a smile on my face. I tried to play it down, but when you're bursting with excitement, it's hard to conceal. Privately, I now realize John sensed something was going on behind his back.

Mark and I continued meeting, but both of us were adamant we were not about to leave our partners. As our relationship reached six months, the conversation changed. Mark started talking about a future that included me. I was frightened. Did I want that? Could I handle the pain of a breakup with John? The answer was I didn't know. I was confused.

Mark took a business trip to Seattle. "I'm going to miss you like crazy, but I'll be back before you know it," he assured. I missed him, but we spoke or Facetimed every day. Even on the other side of the world, he could not stop thinking about me.

In our last exchange, he said: "Miss you, Gorgeous Girl."

Mark returned with a gift—a £100 bottle of Chanel. I was over the moon. I gave him a thank-you kiss. He smiled, "Lou (his wife) didn't even get out of the chair when I came home, hadn't cooked any dinner, and never thanked me for her perfume."

"Well, I'm grateful, and unlike Lou, I do appreciate your lovely gesture. Thank you."

Was that true? Had Lou given him a frosty reception? He had no reason to lie. Perhaps she had fallen out of love with him? According to Mark, they despised one another and were only together for the sake of their kids. I only knew his version of events.

I started telling myself, "Maybe one day, things might be more than a stolen kiss in the dark." But deep down, I didn't know what I wanted.

~

The summer holidays arrived; Mark and I were disappointed because it meant we couldn't meet. Mark and his family set off to Florida. John, myself and the kids flew to Greece. Despite the different time zones, we messaged every moment we could. "Miss you, Gorgeous girl. Can't wait to see you again."

Ironically, the time spent with my family that summer made me realize that, despite my connection and attraction to Mark, I wanted my marriage to work. I know that sounds crazy, but it's the way I felt.

I took John to the bar alone, and we had a heart to heart chat. "I want things to change," I said. "I miss us. Football and friends have taken over our lives. I want more family and us time." John agreed and then went straight back to boys' sports and left Emily and me at the pool.

That was the make or break moment about whether to fight for our marriage or not. John's actions were the answer. He didn't get how I felt.

Frustrated, angry, and depressed, I confided in my friend, Veronica, who was holidaying with us. I was worried my tale would be too shocking, but she shocked me. She told me she had snorted more than her fair share of cocaine with another friend, Nicky, then flirted with a stranger at a live music night in nearby Weston. She had given the stranger her number, and he had messaged her secretly. Veronica explained she "was thinking" of meeting in secret with him again. Her confession confirmed my perception of other people's relationships; no one was perfect, and everyone hid lies behind closed doors.

I decided Veronica's secret was Veronica's secret. The best thing I could do, as a good friend, was never ask what happened.

18.

GOODBYE, WANKER!

"Nothing lasts forever. Forever is a lie. All we have is what's between hello and goodbye."

— Anonymous

2016…

Sometimes, life is just a pile of poop.

I'd found a lump in my breast. The National Health Service (NHS) system required a six-week wait before a scan. It was like awaiting a death sentence. I was frightened. Fortunately, John's medical cover allowed me to go private at a cost, in around ten days. Even that felt like a ten-year wait to see if I was going to die. With my luck, I was certain the results would be dreadful.

John tried to be understanding; keep me calm. He knew my emotions ran rampant at the first hint of difficulty. I had to keep smiling and act normal, so I didn't upset the kids. I began thinking about my funeral and having to tell my children Mummy was going to leave them and go to heaven. That broke me.

Mark was also surprisingly supportive, doing research on herbal medicines and sending me private text links from Florida. For the next ten days, I just shut down. I didn't want to see or speak to anyone. I hid away at home and ignored messages from friends. Perhaps it was my punishment? I deserved it.

~

D-day came. The consultant was cautious. "Mrs. FitzGerald, can't say until we look at the final report, but the indications are that the lump is simply a benign mass." I breathed a bit easier. A few days later, at the follow-up appointment, my specialist delivered great news. "False alarm, just lumpy breast tissue, probably caused by stress." A great weight was taken off my shoulders, replaced by another weight—I'd created the lumpy breast all by myself with all my lies and deceit.

Panic over, John focused even more intensely on gaining a corporate directorship. I started to realize that life was repeating itself, mirroring my time with Will; John's work was more important than *us*. I also continued to wonder about the women at work, the ones he never spoke about, the ones who he socialized with during company outings, and overnight stays in London.

My thought process became snippy, some might even say, quite off the norm. I consciously decided to continue seeing Mark.

~

Mark and I had been apart for six weeks during the summer, and he had said that he couldn't wait for me to be in his arms.

Unexpectedly he drove past me in his car. He had that glint in his eye; I mirrored it. He rolled down the window. I wanted to jump in the passenger seat and drive away.

"God, you look amazing! I can't wait to spend time with you! Have a little surprise."

The surprise turned out to be a memorable stay away at a Maidenhead hotel in Berkshire, including a romantic dinner by the river at the sleek and contemporary, Boulters Brasserie. It was two hours from home, far enough away from any prying eyes. The buzz and thrill of the evening were like nothing I had ever experienced. Terrible as it may sound, I could now see why so many of my friends had been having affairs behind their partner's back.

~

Our night away was magical. We walked and talked; fingers interlaced as we ambled alongside the river, hearing its gentle rush against the muddy banks. I felt the warmth of his touch; my hand encased inside his with a muscular grip that made my body come alive. Without warning, he halted our footsteps, stared into my eyes and placed his tender lips on mine. His hand slid to the small of my back, pulling me close. At that moment, everything around us disappeared. The hum of the bustling traffic, the low-swooping birds gliding over the rippling water, the rush-hour workers heading home for the day. It felt safe; we didn't have a care in the world. We were inside our perfect bubble with no distractions.

Although we'd had secret lunches, this was our first "proper" date. "Perfect woman, perfect date, perfect memory," beamed Mark in the moonlight. We held hands in front of large picture windows watching the quaint narrow boats sail past the expensive riverside houses.

Butterflies swarmed when his eyes caressed mine. His warm fingers traced my fingertips as we shared chorizo scotch eggs with tarragon, and indulged in an expensive bottle of red. We both felt a spark and exchanged nervous smiles. It was a pivotal moment, and I felt like the luckiest girl in the world. I felt alive again. I was Mark's "gorgeous girl."

I didn't feel guilty about Mark's wife, Lou, because *he told me* she detested him, and *I was certain* John didn't want me either. I was certain he'd fallen out of love with me. After all, he was away with football again; he had flown to France with his mates!

I rationalized, why could I not be allowed some happiness? I know what I did was wrong, but I needed to smile again. Another important lesson learned; *there is no proper excuse for improper indiscretion. Ever.*

~

Days later, the shit hit the fan! John knew! He'd been on my phone and seen the messages. "Hope Fatboy42 was worth it," he said.

Those words sliced me in two. I nearly collapsed on the spot, but I couldn't deny it.

My world crumbled; the walls crashed down. I wanted to vomit. Everyone else had gotten away with their flings, not me. I'd been caught out. I was frantic. John and I spoke privately. "How could you do this to me?' he said.

I told him it was the wrong thing to do; that I was sorry. "You were once my world, my teenage sweetheart, my best friend, and soulmate. But I barely see you now. I was lonely, but I know that's no excuse."

"You've broken our trust," he replied.

I had to say what needed to be said. "This is not all about you. I deserve to be treated better, instead of always being last. You're never home and are always socializing with other women. I thought you were cheating on me." John didn't utter a word. To me, that said it all.

Tensions were at a boiling point. We agreed to put on a brave face while we sorted things out.

~

John, embarrassed by the turn of events, promised he wouldn't confront Mark, or tell his wife, Lou. But how could I be sure? If the shoe were on the other foot, I would have.

I frantically messaged Mark to tell him John knew. I violated the one rule Mark and I had agreed: no calls or texts on the weekend. Mark responded by text with one lousy word, "Goodbye." He had decided to protect himself. What a wanker! (a contemptible person).

Mark then threw me under the bus, telling Lou about the minor indiscretion. I don't know what was said, but I'm certain the blame was placed on me. He wouldn't have admitted to initiating the chase.

We messaged a few times after that, both of us admitting that what we'd done was wrong and had caused nothing but pain. Had we not been caught out, I'm certain it would have been a whole other story.

Even though Mark bailed on me, I felt Lou deserved an apology. I decided to do it face to face. I'd stolen the heart of her husband of some 15 years. I should say sorry. As I stood in the carpark, my stomach churned. Lou spoke calmly, "It was obvious it was you. Mark talked about you all the time, and you were always walking dogs together. He should never have shat on his doorstep!"

I explained that while it made no difference, she should know that Mark did the chasing. "He pursued me for months. Against my better judgment, I relented."

She stared scornfully. Without thinking, I blurted: "We should never have let it go on so long."

She asked, "How long?"

I told her the truth, "Seven months."

"You're telling me this went on for seven months, and John never confronted my husband?

"Yes."

"So, you're also a liar!" she responded defensively.

Lou was unhinged; her neat little world had just crumbled. She knew Mark had lied to her about the true extent of the fling, but he was not about to admit to a seven-month affair. I expect he told Lou what she wanted to hear, "It was a silly dalliance that happened just once."

As Lou stood staring angrily, I did something stupid—I complimented her on her outfit—maybe it was my nerves, I don't know.

I fully deserved her wrath, but I was terrified for months that she would turn up on my doorstep.

I never heard from Mark again. But since he had treated me like utter shit, I decided to leave left a parting memento on Mark's doorstep—the £100 bottle of perfume he gave me. Then I texted him saying I'd returned it. Mark went nuts. "Move it now!" his text screamed. "Throw it in the dog poo bin." I realized he didn't know me—I don't respond well to orders from anyone.

That evening I sat alone, wondering. Had I lost everything important on my journey from disappointment to depression to despair? Was I at rock bottom? I wondered was it time for this lost soul to say *no mas.*

19.

THAT FIRST TIME

"Sometimes life pushes us to our limits because God only gives his toughest battles to his strongest soldiers."
— Ankita Chakraborty

2016…

When you lose control of your mind, a demonic force enters to take you on a trip to hell!

I put on my boots and left the house in my pajamas as tears streamed down my cheeks. I got in the car and started to drive somewhere, anywhere.

My head ached. I had a massive migraine filled with emotion; anger, hate, sadness, grief, and remorse. The pain was unbearable. I just wanted it to stop. I became hysterical and could barely see the road ahead through my watery eyes. I had no clue what I was doing, I just raced, drove towards the coast at Sand Bay, slamming my foot on the accelerator, negotiating the winding, country roads.

Soon, I was surrounded by wilderness. My speedometer read 90 mph. Twigs snapped against my windows like police batons trying to deter me. Hedges scraped the car's exterior. I was prepared for a certain massive collision. I closed my eyes and released my grip on the steering wheel as the car screeched around a blind bend in the road.

Images of John and the children flashed through my mind. I realized I couldn't kill myself—not that way. The images would be too gruesome, bloody. It was not the way I wanted to be remembered.

I decided to keep driving. The speedometer slowed to 50 mph, although my foot remained glued to the accelerator. Now, a mass of perspiration, I let the devil take charge. Low-moving dark clouds covered the full moon in complete darkness. My car came to a full stop. Strong sea breezes rocked the car, demanding I get out.

I started walking toward the sea; my boots dragged over the dunes. I felt like I had 50-pound weights around each ankle. I stumbled again and again on the uneven ground as spikes of the damp seaweeds, pierced my palms. I raised the coat collar around my neck and continued my march to the sea.

In the middle of my quest, the cell phone tucked deep in my pocket began to vibrate. I knew it was John. I longed to say one final goodbye, but I was afraid he'd talk me out of killing myself. I didn't want that! I had made so many bad choices; I didn't deserve redemption. I wanted everything to be over and the pain I felt to go.

Wave after wave crashed against the rocks, spitting froth in my face. I could feel their raw power dragging me into the sea. Powerful winds shortened every breath. About knee-high, the angry winds whipped my wet hair strands across my face, slapping my cheeks, again and again.

I had fallen for Mark's charm, then was discarded like trash as he protected his own sorry arse. As for John, he had marginalized me by always putting me last, did he deserve a goodbye? The phone just kept vibrating. I was paralyzed. My cries echoed through the bay. I took the mobile out of my pocket. The screen illuminated like a flashlight directing me further out to sea. I could see the thunderous waves pounding the cliffs.

The phone stopped vibrating. I closed my eyes. My numb body was now waist-high in the inky black ocean. It wouldn't be long before I would be sucked under by the strong currents. The phone again vibrated. The screen illuminated. It was a voicemail from John. Standing in the water, I decided I did want to hear his voice one last time. I pressed the phone against my damp hair, closed my eyes, and listened. John's voice begged me to come home. "I've made mistakes, you've made mistakes. It doesn't matter. Come home, and we can work things out."

My mind raced. What should I do? Was it possible John might still love me despite everything?

I decided to turn around and to head back to shore. My legs gave way; it was now a struggle between the angry sea and me. I managed a few steps. The waves receded; I dug my hands into the sand for traction. The waves returned and tugged again. I hung on for dear life. My mouth was filled with salt water and sand. The waves again receded, I mustered all my strength to rise and run for the safety of the dry shore.

Moments later, I sat on the sand, shivering, physically exhausted. My mind was flooded with dark questions.

Would pictures of my body dragged from the sea and plucked out by lifeboat crews have been more horrific than an auto crash?

Suppose my dreaded Coastguard Mark recovered my body. Would he realize his vile behavior was a major reason for my suicide? Would his sleazy face even care?

Then there was John, my parents, and the kids. How would they deal with the final image of a woman who had gone momentarily mad?

I felt pathetic; I didn't have answers, only questions. And, I didn't even have the guts to kill myself. I couldn't even get that right. I was a complete failure. I slumped back behind the wheel, hypothermic. I don't recall the drive home.

When I pulled onto the driveway, John stood aghast at my drenched, filthy body with sand-filled boots.

The children heard voices and appeared at the top of the stairs peering down. John told them to go back to bed. They did as they were told. John hugged me, and my tears fell. He was grateful that I'd come back and hadn't done something stupid. Not a word was exchanged. Neither of us knew what to say. I climbed the stairs, changed my pyjamas and fell asleep exhausted.

When I woke, John had left for work. He'd decided to carry on life as normal. That's what he did best, ignoring what was before him. I decided to follow his lead by pretending to play mum. Since the kids had no idea what had happened the night before, I painted on a fake smile, got them ready for school, made breakfast and lunchboxes and took them to school.

~

When I returned home, I fell apart. I collapsed on the hallway floor and cried until no more tears could flow. I remember climbing the stairs, sitting in my office, and staring at the walls. Finally, I decided to call two friends to confide in them about Mark. I didn't have the guts to talk about my suicide attempt. I wanted to forget it had ever occurred. I've never told a soul to this day, not even my parents. I was too ashamed that I'd contemplated abandoning my entire family.

Mary wasn't surprised. She knew how I'd felt for a very long time. I always confided in her like she was my sister.

"Vicki, I know you've been unhappy for years. I wish I were closer to be there for you. You're a strong, capable woman. It will all work out."

Anna was the opposite; blunt. "At the end of the day, you did what you did," she scorned, as though she was little Miss Perfect. She seemed to forget her own, numerous immoral actions.

After that moment, a distance grew between us. I know why; Anna didn't want me to expose her dirty secrets. Had I, two people would be dead, of that I'm certain.

Anna was also obedient, she did what she was told by her husband, to avoid a violent encounter. I'd supported her through such times, yet she could not return the favor. Protecting her sordid secrets, was far more important, than being a shoulder to her best friend.

All I knew was her friendship was the least of my concerns. I wanted to try to fix our flawed marriage. I didn't want this to be the end of the road.

Despite everything, both of our actions, I still loved John. I knew it wouldn't be easy; it wasn't a case of clicking my fingers and making everything normal. I had to take the initiative to make things right.

I cried on Mum's shoulder as I explained, "John and I need time to try and fix our marriage, somewhere far away from here."

Mum said she and Dad would take care of the kids for however long it took. "We don't want your marriage to be over. It wouldn't be fair to the children, and our family."

I spoke at length to John. Told him that I didn't want this to be the end and I was prepared to fight for us, reunite us as one. John agreed a long weekend hiding away to sort things out privately seemed like the best option.

"We need to get far away from here," I said.

John responded, "I agree, where do you want to go?"

"Anywhere," I said.

We jumped on a plane and traveled 1,335 miles to the seaside resort of Alicante, Spain, to try to pick up the pieces and save our broken marriage.

20.

STARTING OVER, AGAIN

"We cannot escape tragedy. It is like grasping at the sun, trying to catch air. We must take one step at-a-time. Keep going."

— Ace Antonio Hall

2016…

Everyone makes mistakes in life, but that doesn't mean they have to pay for them for the rest of their life.

One thing was certain. John and I knew we wanted to give us another chance; otherwise, we wouldn't have got on the plane.

As we sat buckled on the runway preparing for take-off, I realized starting over would be a lot more difficult than it sounded.

I thought about my preoccupation with the dumb choices, my versions of the truth, and my bizarre rationalizations.

Despite my incoherent fragility, I had made a definitive choice; I wanted to live and mend our broken hearts. I also needed to focus on healing myself emotionally. I needed to answer the question, what did I want out of life?

I closed my eyes and imagined Gramps was by my side offering advice—"love of family is everything." Suddenly, everything was crystal clear. All I ever wanted was John's love, affection, and attention. I didn't care about the lavish life he provided with luxury holidays. I just wanted him to be a more loving husband and for us to have a normal family, whatever that means in today's upside-down world.

I would be less than honest if I didn't admit that part of me wanted to expose the dirty secrets of those who wronged me, but revenge rarely solves anything. Eventually, all their dirty little infidelities will be exposed because karma is wicked, and the truth always comes out in the end.

Deep down, those people know the pain they have created in my life and what they've done to those who they love. It's a guilt they will carry with them, as I do for the rest of their lives. For me, that is more than enough.

~

Heading off on holiday together was awkward. In the space of a few days, we'd fought, our marriage was in question, and I'd tried to kill myself. Yet madly, we were side by side and heading to Spain.

Barely speaking, we got off the plane and checked into a hotel. We then just went out as though we were tourists on a "normal" holiday.

At first, we avoided "the" conversation, boarding the replica Santisima Trinidad pirate ship, and posted photos online (to appear normal). It was odd, looking back, both of us trying to show an interest in the ship and its treasures. I suppose we were avoiding the discussion that we needed to have.

We explored Alicante further, ate Tapas, drank beer and sangria with the sun on our faces. Perhaps we wanted to see if we could still be a couple and enjoy each other's company. Or neither of us wanted to be the first to bring it up.

After more sangria and cerveza, I eventually mustered the courage to talk. "I never loved Mark; I was just lonely," I confessed.

"Why him?"

"It just happened. He chased me. I was fed up with being on my own, and I thought you'd cheated on me with those other women."

There was silence. If my suspicions were correct, John was not going to admit to it. The truth is, I didn't want to know the answer; it would have added to the torment and would make no difference now.

I was to shield all the blame, and I was prepared to do that if it meant we would remain as a family. It was all I ever wanted. Life happens; people change and can betray those that they love most; friends as well as partners.

"I begged you to pay me more attention and cut down on the football, time and time again. You ignored me. I thought you didn't love me anymore."

I could see the hurt in John's eyes. I think he finally realized how miserable he'd made me feel and that he'd pushed me away. That upset him too. We were both sad.

"I don't want us to end," I insisted.

"Neither do I," replied John

"I do love you, John."

"I love you, too."

The conversion ended. John wanted to move on, so did I. He didn't want to talk about it anymore. Communication was never his strong point, perhaps that's why we ended up where we did. We would focus on building a better future and not dwell on past mistakes.

We would have fun, too, fun together for a change. Dressed to impress in a dress and heels, John in a nice shirt, we visited a casino in the marina. I'd never been to a casino. I found it exciting gambling on an iPad around a table. John was smirking because I kept winning, which pissed off the male players. Hurt male pride and all that! My luck didn't stay; I lost my winnings. It didn't matter because we were experiencing something new together, and we both had smiles on our faces that had been absent for so very long.

I didn't want the trip to end. It reminded me of our early years holidaying in Sa Coma, Corfu, and Turkey before the kids were born. The days when we'd lie carefree on a beach when he'd sing and serenade me and smile. And that's what we did next. We sunbathed side by side. The warmth of the sun on my face was comforting. It felt as though God was telling me everything was going to be alright.

I didn't want our journey to end. I longed to reignite the spark. Bring back who we used to be. I wanted to be the girl with whom John fell in love with. And, I wanted him to remember the promise that he'd made: *"I'll always love you, one day you'll realize how much, and I will make you happy, happier than ever before."* But a lot had happened; we were not kids' anymore, and we had responsibilities.

As John and I talked that weekend together, our discussion became open and honest; important truths were recognized.

- We were both lost and broken. I'd shattered his heart; he'd fractured mine with abandonment.
- John and I were still soulmates and best friends. Neither of us wanted our marriage to end.
- Mark was a creep. He didn't deserve my attention.
- John needed to create balance in his life; we needed more shared experiences.
- We had taken our love for granted. The cracks in our once perfect world were self-evident.
- We both loved our children without reservation.

It was time came to return home. As we boarded the plane, I was overwhelmed with the thought of real life. We both sat in silence the entire trip. As the plane landed, I stared out of the window and cried, my tears mirroring the rain droplets on the glass.

I shielded John from my tears and self-doubt. Could all that had transpired be neatly brushed under the carpet and forgotten? I tried to convince myself it could, but deep down I knew I was lying to myself. Sadly, I had become good at doing that; but the fact is, *some things can never be forgotten.*

21.
FRIENDS ARE FOREVER, SOMETIMES

"I thought I knew the world, I thought I knew myself, I thought I knew my best friend, but I knew nothing at all."
— Estrella DeMadrigal

May 2017…

Sometimes friends just aren't all they cracked up to be.

Lara had taken her car into the garage to be serviced and needed a ride home. As any good friend, would, I agreed to pick her up in my new black Volkswagen Polo and drive her home until her vehicle was ready the next day.

Lara was hungover—she had been having ongoing problems since splitting with her husband and was drinking heavily. She said, "Could we please stop for some hangover food?" We chuckled a bit, then I stopped at the McDonald's drive-through and got her a quarter pounder with cheese and a Coke. From there, we continued home.

As I drove up Lara's road, my car began to rev, the engine roared, and the car picked up speed.

"What the hell are you doing?" screeched Lara.

"It's not me; something's not right with the car!"

I slammed my foot on the brake pedal. There was no response. The car kept rolling. While we weren't going fast, my bumper hit the brickwork on the extension to her home. I was horrified.

"What the fuck was that," Lara asked, clinging to her McDonald's Coke cup.

"You alright?" I asked.

"Yeah, that was weird!" said Lara.

I apologized "The brakes wouldn't hold, I'm so sorry."

Lara looked in the mirror and smiled. The drink had splattered everywhere. "At least my face enjoyed the Coke." We both laughed.

We got out to inspect the damage. My bumper was scratched, her bricks cracked. Other than that, we were both completely fine.

~

It was my responsibility to make things right with Lara's home. I obtained the contact details of a builder friend to come and quote the house repair work. It turned out her ex-husband had built the extension without regard for building regulations. So instead of fixing some cracks, the entire extension needed redoing at a cost of £4k, which my insurers paid. Lara loved it— her faulty, non-conforming extension would be fixed, and she would get a new front door too.

The dealer took my car for a few days. "We cannot find a single fault with the car," said the dealer. "But we've replaced the bumper and sensors."

Only the car was not fixed, and my brakes soon failed again. To avoid crashing into a car in front, this time I swerved to the left. Luckily, I narrowly avoided the car. I drove to the garage and told them the same fault had occurred. "This car's a death trap," I complained.

The dealer refused to replace the car. They did not want to leave themselves open to a liability claim. Without my approval, they quickly replaced the brake master cylinder system and eliminated any possible evidence by destroying the old parts. I was then given a hideous, poo brown VW hire car.

I rowed with VW for a year to get out of the car lease. I was not willing to put myself or the kids at risk. Eventually, they agreed.

~

A week after the initial accident at Lara's, I'd been invited for a girl's night. Lara, Anna, and I were dancing in Lara's kitchen, drinking some Prosecco, and generally having a fun time. Lara thought it would be funny to have her teenage daughter teach us a provocative dance move called the "slut drop." (A dance move that involved dropping to the floor seductively and rising back up).

We were laughing ourselves silly. It was not a move women of our age should be attempting, but it was fun behind closed doors.

After slugging down her prosecco, Lara blurted out of the blue. "I'm going to sue your insurance company!"

"What for?" I asked.

"Personal injury in the automobile accident."

"You must be joking," I replied. "You weren't even injured."

Lara shrugged her shoulders. "Doesn't matter."

"Dreadful," I responded. "Who would sue their best friend?"

"I'm not," said Lara. "I'm suing your insurance company."

"But your fraudulent claim could increase my premiums."

Lara smiled and carried on dancing. The conversation ended. I wondered if she was merely joking, but an uneasy feeling simmered in my stomach. I wondered would she really do that to one of her best friends.

22.

DEVIL IN DISGUISE

"That which does not kill us, makes us stronger."
— Friedrich Nietzsche

2017…

Friends that use rumors against friends are evil.

Life was going on. John surprised me by booking a family holiday to Jamaica just before Christmas. My self-doubt was unfounded! He wanted to try again. Jamaica was our special place, one which we all held fondly in our hearts.

I decided to reciprocate with a surprise of my own. I wanted him to know he was still "my man." I'd ask him to renew our wedding vows over a moonlight dinner on the beach with the sound of gently rolling waves in the background.

I put my heart on the line, secretly praying that I wasn't about to make a fool of myself. "John, will you marry me again?"

"Yes," he replied, just as the kids emerged and interrupted the romantic moment.

"Guess what, children,' I announced, "Mum and Dad are getting married again." The kids were delighted and wanted to be part of the wedding celebrations.

"Can I get a bridesmaid dress?" Emily quizzed eagerly. "Of course," I smiled. The renewal vows meant the turmoil of the past few years could be forgotten, and we could start again.

We had been married for 13 years. I told myself 13 was unlucky. John, "it's a bad omen to renew our marriage vows on a bad number." I suggested we plan the ceremony for our 15th anniversary.

"I think that's a bit silly, being so superstitious," smiled John, "but if that's what makes you happy."

The trip was magical, a bonding moment for us all. I longed to be a perfect little family again and had planned a series of adventures to bring us all closer together, rather than splitting into boy and girl teams.

In what I can only describe as one of the best days of my life, we sailed down the Black River feeding crocodiles, visited a sanctuary and held a baby crocodile, then zip wired through the tropical jungles over seven waterfalls at YS Falls, one of Jamaica's finest natural attractions.

"Again, again," Emily screeched as she glided over the final waterfall. There were smiles all around. We genuinely were having the time of our lives.

The fun didn't stop there, we swung on ropes into the natural rock pools and explored the lush gardens, before heading to our final destination; Floyds Pelican bar; a driftwood stilted shack ¾ mile out to sea in St Elizabeth.

We hired a rickety boat and sailed out for 20 minutes to the coolest bar in the world. We hung out with the locals, enjoyed a rum cocktail, swam in the sea, and had our names engraved on the driftwood floor. To me, it was a permanent reminder that the FitzGerald family were reunited and happier than ever before.

Back home, John and I started to make time for each other. We went on date nights and tried to rekindle our teenage love.

He agreed that drinking with friends had ruined us, and we would reduce the nights spent socializing with them. He would smile and say, "We've let friends come first before. Those days are over."

Promises were made. John would take on an assistant football coach and cut down the tournaments. He also agreed do more things as a family. And, we began to refuse numerous social invites, until our friends got the message. It all seemed too good to be true. It was.

~

Our new plan saved us for a while. Life was good. I told my best friend, Mary, we were better than ever.

"You seem really happy," Mary said, smiling, as we ate lunch.

"I'm glad all this has happened," I replied. Mary looked confused.

"If anything, it's brought us closer than ever. We are spending more time together; we're back to snuggling on the sofa. Life is good again." I could feel my face beaming.

I was certain we had begun to have pushed the bad memories aside and would grow old together. I wanted that with every inch of me. I loved John deeply.

John made his position clear about Mark, "So long as no one finds out, I can forget it." I agreed. I wanted to bury him (literally) and my mum, and best friends, Lara and Mary, could be trusted to keep it secret. So, for the next 18 months, we worked hard at being a happy family again.

~

Old habits die hard—the promises never materialised. An assistant coach was never appointed. Football commitments continued unabated. We were back to split boy and girl teams and John moved back to his reclining chair at the opposite end of the lounge with his phone on silent, facedown. I felt sick and wondered whether revenge was on the cards.

John's work continued to take him to London, and there were new frequent flights to the Isle of Man. He remained consumed with being promoted to director.

Every time I mentioned the vow renewal when he was home, it was disregarded. I wondered if he was having second thoughts and started to feel rejected, again. Perhaps it was too much too soon. I should never have proposed. I made a complete fool of myself.

Then there were the drinking nights with the friends. They continued to be a fixture into our lives—big mistake.

One evening, over a few glasses of wine at my house, I shared my inner thoughts with one of my closest friends Lara, who I trusted with my life. I didn't know at the time; Lara had already stabbed a knife right in my back and divulged our secret.

~

Days later, I was sharing a glass of wine with Anna—her husband, Tom, and John were friends. She was chatting about some local gossip. I feigned surprise that something like that would happen in our quiet little community. Big mistake! Anna looked me straight in the eye and said, "I know everything about Fatboy42."

I was stunned. "Lara told me all about you and Mark. Lara said she was surprised you had the guts to admit such and apologize to Mark's wife face-to-face."

I felt sick. I wanted the world to swallow me up whole. I was embarrassed, consumed by rage and feared the gossip would spread at warp speed. Perhaps, even more importantly, if Anna knew, then Tom probably knew. John would be furious with me that our friends knew our private business.

My world was unraveling—again. There are no words that adequately describe my inner turmoil. I was frightened to death that John would leave me for good this time.

After Anna left, I sat by the fireplace wondering: how could Lara betray me? I'd picked her off the floor during her messy separation from Craig. And, I remained a loyal friend and cheerleader when she was depressed and too drunk to care for her kids. I even took her son to school in my son's spare uniform when she was too hungover to get out of bed.

Then there were promiscuous moments when Lara fell completely off the rails. She was hooking up with countless men through dating apps, and confessed, "I think I've become a sex addict." I coached her through those dark moments, never once sharing her secrets.

I was far from perfect; I'd sinned. But it was inconceivable Lara would reveal my Mark mistake to Anna. Friends confide, they share their secrets, heartaches and upsets. I'd been a great friend, had been at Lara's and Anna's side through thick and thin. Yet, Lara wasn't so honest, and had gossiped behind my back. That hurt. She betrayed me—our friendship would never be the same again. Whatever the reason, Lara knowingly decided to toss me in the trash heap. Perhaps she wanted my life to fall apart like hers. Who knows?

I made a huge decision; ended our friendship. I would never forgive her for breaking my trust. And I knew I could never confide in her again. She had meant the world to me. My sweet Lara turned out to be the devil in disguise.

23.

POTTY PEOPLE

"Style is knowing who you are, what you want to say, and not giving a damn."

— Orson Welles

2017…

Once you are the subject of nasty gossip by potty people (those who use crude language), it hurts like a knife to the gut and the scars don't heal.

No matter how much it hurts to lose a friendship, there are true friends who remain at your side. Veronica and Ryan remained close friends with John and me. We frequently socialized and went on summer holidays together to Greece and Turkey.

Veronica was eleven years older than me and dressed mumsy, while Ryan had a bit of an untimely potty mouth and made it his business to flirt with any woman with a pulse. She turned a blind eye.

During May Bank Holiday, Ryan had become inebriated at a BBQ in our house. He slinked up behind me, and whispered, "I bet you're *a good fuck*. I'd like to fuck you, just once. Veronica and John never need know. We could do it on holiday!"

I glared sternly then walked away disgusted. Naïvely, I blamed Ryan's potty mouth on the bottle of rum he had been chugging down. I was too horrified to tell Veronica, but I did tell John.

He laughed, saying: "Ryan won't even remember what he said tomorrow morning." I was surprised John was so calm. I, on the other hand, was mortified and had wanted John to confront him. He didn't.

Afterwards, I kept a distance, pondering over whether I should tell Veronica, she was my friend after all. But John said it was better to forget about it and treat it as a drunken joke. There was no point in causing them marital problems.

Ryan kept his eye on me at the next social gathering; I could feel his eyes follow me. I ignored him. I never found Ryan remotely attractive; he was an unpolished middle-class bloke. John was the love of my life.

He noticed I was quiet around him and had the nerve to ask, "Are you okay? Is anything wrong?" He was red faced. I could tell he'd remembered the inappropriate suggestion. "I'm fine," I answered and walked away.

I wanted to say, "I'm disgusted by you." But I didn't. Some things are better left alone. I remained upset and felt very uncomfortable. We had gone from friends sharing great times, to me wanting to avoid him at all costs.

The feeling lingered. Our mutual friend Anna asked me if everything was okay; I made another big mistake and told her about the inebriated comment. "Oh God, what did John say?" she asked.

"He told me to forget it and put it down to drunken behaviour. Should I tell Veronica? I don't know what to do." Anna was flippant. "Just forget it. He was hammered (drunk)."

I took their advice. I'd shield Veronica from the truth and spare her any heartache. Isn't that what good friends do? Looking back, that was the wrong decision. If I'd made her aware of the crude advance, things may have turned out differently between Veronica and me.

~

We went on our Turkish holiday, booked some months earlier. I felt extremely uncomfortable and did my upmost to avoid being around Ryan, without John being present. I'd notice him frequently staring at me in my bikini and it made my stomach turn. And when I'd get in the pool with the kids, he'd follow. But I still felt it was best to ignore his behaviour and enjoy the holiday with my children.

Just months after we returned from the holiday, Ryan got his finger caught in the cookie jar. Veronica discovered Ryan was 'sexting' with her best friend, Chloe. All the messages he'd been sending were coming through on the iPad at home, which their child had read.

Veronica was furious that her oldest school friend could cheat with her husband. While Veronica was one of my closest friends, I could see why Ryan might stray—Veronica frequently demeaned him in public like a child.

It was clear their love had died; they were just one of those couples staying together for their child.

~

Out of the blue, Ryan called. "Veronica's on a rampage. She's accused me of having secret liaisons with all of her friends, including you!"

I was dumbstruck. "That's ridiculous," I screeched, feeling hurt.

"I'll call her right now and set the record straight!"

"No, don't. She doesn't even know that I've called you."

I was put in another terribly awkward situation thanks to Ryan.

John was furious with Veronica's wicked accusation. He knew, despite the past, and Ryan's aggressive advances at our BBQ, that I would never entertain the idea of relations with Ryan, but that didn't stop me from feeling humiliated and embarrassed.

A few days later, Veronica and I met face to face. "I've caught Ryan sexting with Chloe, saying some of the most disgusting things."

I pretended that I wasn't aware. "I'm sorry to hear that. Sadly, that's what some men do for attention," I said, trying to calm her down. "It was probably nothing physical."

"How can I be sure?" she said, "Suppose John was sexting with me; would you say the same thing? The bastard's made a mockery of our marriage. How could a friend do that to me?"

I didn't like her accusatory tone or her questioning stare. I couldn't hold back. "Listen, Ryan is in the wrong and has betrayed you, as has Chloe, but I understand you also believe he's been hooking up with all of your friends, including me. I would never betray you!"

Veronica looked horrified. I explained that I'd received a call from Ryan, informing me of the whole sordid affair and her suggestion that I could stray with him. I was not about to be brought into their mess.

"I'd never do anything to damage our relationship and I don't take kindly to the suggestion."

"My head is a mess. I just can't believe it. Chloe was my best friend since school. I shouldn't assume all my friends are guilty."

"No, you shouldn't!"

Apparently, Veronica had examined all his texts. Two on his phone were from me, outlining holiday arrangements (her phone didn't work abroad). The third was in relation to a post-holiday curry night for us all, but she assumed we were having a secret liaison. It was ridiculous.

Never once did Veronica apologize for her tawdry accusation. I'd wanted to tell her about the BBQ comment, so she could see what her husband was really like, but she was already so upset, I spared her further pain.

~

Anna could tell I wasn't myself and asked why I seemed down. Over a few glasses of prosecco, I told her about Veronica's accusation. It had hurt terribly. People were already spreading rumours and I was adamant that I wanted my name cleared. I did not want to be associated with Ryan's sordid behaviour—he repulsed me.

I was still unsure whether now was the time to tell her about the BBQ. "I'd leave it and give her time to cool down," Anna said. She was right, they had serious problems that they should resolve without any interference and I didn't want to be labelled a homewrecker.

~

We retreated to Barbados as a family just before Christmas, staying where Simon Cowell's luxury yacht was moored. It was idyllic.

After the fun activities experienced in Jamaica, I wanted us to enjoy some more family fun and build memories to last a lifetime. The four of us swam with turtles, took Jeep Safaris around the island, ate waterfront dinners at the locally famous Oistins Fish Fry, and watched the monkeys run around the beach.

We were having a wonderful time. John and I were focusing on our own lives. I'd even posted a picture of us on the beach, captioned: "I cannot wait to marry this man again!" And, I'd meant every word.

A few days before we returned, Veronica's close relatives were involved in an accident. Despite being in the Caribbean, and still not having received an apology from Veronica, I sent her flowers to cheer her up. I was determined to remain a kind, loyal friend.

For Christmas, I'd also created a photo book of our many holiday snaps as a gift. I'd tried to make an effort. Veronica should have been the one begging for forgiveness, but she didn't, not once.

~

Things between us finally started to feel normal again. Veronica made Emily a birthday cake for her 9th birthday in January—perhaps, that was her way of saying sorry. The party was a success. The next week was hectic, so I sent a short message apologizing for not being in contact.

Her vile response knocked me for six. "Don't ever contact me again. Our friendship is over. I know you've been talking about me behind my back! I'm sick and tired of people discussing my marriage."

I was shocked. I hadn't spoken of their marital issues, only of the accusation with Anna (in order to get another opinion.) I assume Anna must have said something to Veronica at the birthday party. I was also aware that our old neighbour, Maria, was gossiping behind Veronica's back, telling us both different stories and stirring the pot.

I tried to defend myself via text. I was the innocent party (this time around). Veronica chose to shut me down and listen to others. Our friendship became more collateral damage in the continuing soap opera of my life. My friendships were falling like dominos; I'd now lost two friends. Only this time around, I was heartbroken by the loss.

~

The Mark affair, coupled with the accusation from my potty-mouth friends, dredged up the past. John was equally fed up with the whole saga. He became quiet and distant. John's exit plan was to continue to make work his obsession and first love, and his passion for football a close second. The rest he'd figure out in time. Despite all the drama, he remained a kind, loving father.

My parents believed he was a model husband, and that much of our martial chaos was self-inflicted. It's a shame they never took the time to listen to their daughter's version of events. There are always two sides to every story and aspects of our marriage, which I've never disclosed to them.

I learned another lesson: *always tell the truth, even if it hurts those you care about, because one day, it will come out, twisted along the way.*

24.

THE DAY OUR MUSIC DIED

"Something touched me deep inside, the day the music died."

— Don McLean

2018...

No matter how much you want something to change, fate already decided your future.

After the Lara incident and the Potty People fiasco, life continued to unwind—at a quickening pace.

The tender cuddles on the sofa were gone. John moved back to his man's chair in the corner. His phone was always on silent or face down. I hated it.

I was certain John had something to hide. I'd been there and knew the tricks. He insisted my accusations were a "figment of my fertile imagination." He didn't want to answer calls in the living room; he'd rather call back in private. He also said he was betting on the horses and got periodic notifications.

One night, when the kids were out. I cooked us a rare dinner for two. I tried to chit chat. John didn't respond once. He ate and watched the horses on TV and streamed them on his phone! I thought his behavior was rude; I wouldn't even treat strangers like that.

~

My birthday arrived in March. He'd bought a Champneys Spa stay for two. I thought great, he was trying to make an effort to love me. John informed me he wasn't coming. He'd asked Anna to join me! I wanted to cry.

"I thought you would like to get away from the kids and me," he said. Hardly. "I would have rather we went together," I muttered.

"Anna has already agreed," he replied. I believed John wanted to be rid of me. The spa trip was a good excuse to send me away for a weekend. Or maybe he thought I needed some time out and a chance to relax with a friend.

~

While my marriage was crumbling, I decided to restart my business career. This time as a published author. Years earlier, I'd drafted a novel about the unsolved case of the serial sex attacker, *Adidas Man*. An agent liked it but wanted to reduce the graphic intensity of the sex attacks and add another 40,000 words of detail and content to heighten the suspense of the chase.

I'd just had Emily; I didn't have the time. My book sat in a cupboard for seven years. I told John I wanted to follow my dream: quit PR and write full time.

John had become fabulously successful at work and was fully supportive. We had no financial pressures. He just wanted me to be happy and allowed me to give everything up, so I could finish my book. This time around, I'd matured and conducted extensive research with forensic experts and the police.

Briguella, named after the killer's sinister mask, was published in 2017. John never read it! He was too busy with work and never showed any real interest in my writing. Had he, he would have felt my pain. It's there, in black and white on Amazon and my bookshelf.

Writing had become my world, aside from my children. It meant everything. Writing as a journalist was fun, but creating fiction was magical. I felt this was what I was meant to do in life. I wanted to write from the heart. One day, hopefully, I'd become known and follow in the footsteps of the talented J.K Rowling from Yate, in nearby Bristol. She, too, had a terrible backstory; I was heading down a similar path.

~

Work began on Book Two, *Kill List*, covering a subject that happened to me; drugging. The story soon became my pride and joy. I printed some initial chapters and asked John to have a read, provide some feedback. The chapters sat on the sideboard for three months. I continued writing. He never read them or showed interest.

Some 355 printed pages later, I cried as I wrote the last line. I held the manuscript proudly in my hands; John walked through the door.

"It's finished," I screeched, face beaming as though I'd won the lottery. I felt so very proud of my achievement.

I asked John to take a picture of me holding my manuscript with a glass of Prosecco. I sent the message to my friends and posted it on Facebook. I appeared happy, but deep down, I knew my smile was another lie.

"Well done," muttered John, as he headed to the kitchen to retrieve a beer. After a year of writing, that's all I got from John, a simple "well done". No hug, no excitement, no real interest in my accomplishment. That destroyed any fight I had left in me. I knew *our* music had died.

The dream that we once were, Posh & Becks, had vanished. There was no room in John's life for a woman like me—a woman who craved constant love and attention.

25.

END OF THE ROAD

"Although we've come to the end of the road, still I can't let go. It's unnatural. You belong to me, I belong to you."
— Boyz II Men

2018…

It's easy to look like you're on top of the world; it's quite a bit more difficult to actually be there.

Our marriage was over. We had tried mouth to mouth resuscitation and failed miserably. We were free falling. It hurt badly. Our *friends* Veronica and Ryan put the final nail in the coffin. Their interference and Lara's ensured that my past would never be forgotten.

John left to ponder a future without me. He stayed away for a few days, but our family holiday to luxurious Dubai was looming. We agreed it would be unfair to the kids if we canceled. So we said nothing. We packed our cases and boarded the most luxurious flight we'd ever been on, to the United Emirates.

The children were beyond excited. Little did they know of the heartbreak that John and I were experiencing. It was excruciating.

Our stunning hotel, Jumeriah Mina A 'Salam, was opposite Dubai's most iconic sail-shaped hotel, the Burj Al Arab Jumeirah.

To top it off, the hotel was footballers' paradise, and Matthew's favorite Southampton player was at our pool. That made his dreams come true. I knew escaping to the sun wouldn't fix us, but we would have fun and make final memories of us all together as a family.

~

John sat two sunbeds apart, making it obvious this was our last time. I told him, for the sake of the kids, we needed to make the most of the situation.

He did his part to create an unforgettable experience. We dined in lavish restaurants like the Burj Al Arab Jumeirah, Jumeriah Emirates Towers, Anantara The Palm. We even took Matthew and Emily on terrifying rides at Wadi Wadi water park —I'd never heard them scream so loud! Afterward, we went to the observation deck on the 160th floor of the Burj Khalifa, the world's tallest building. While John and the kids walked around admiring the view, I sat on a bench near a quiet corner window. I closed my eyes and cried. I could hear the wind whistling. It was an eerie experience.

~

Despite the superficial impression we were a cheery family, John and I found time for a private, depressing row. "Too much has happened for too long," he said. "I find it impossible to bury the past."

"I'm sorry, I did love you and still do," I sobbed.

I was not about to take the entire blame for our falling-out. "You've been an equal party to our mess. Not one of the promises you made has ever materialized. Old habits slipped back. The only thing that matters to you is your beloved directorship."

After we finished accusing each other, we decided we would tell the children that Mummy and Daddy didn't love each other anymore as soon as we got home. I took a walk and cried myself to sleep on the beach alone. I didn't care if I was arrested for breaking any laws; I was emotionally spent. The plane ride home felt like the ride to hell.

John found a lovely place to live. He would be leaving us in a week. It all happened so fast; there was no time to let it all sink in. We sat around the dinner table and told the children.

"You can't separate, you both make me feel like the happiest girl in the world," Emily sobbed. It crushed me.

Silence lingered.

John looked me in the eye, waited for me to speak. I shed a tear with every heartbeat. The pain was unbearable, knowing he would never sleep by my side again. John got up, walked out of the door, on us, our family, without so much as another word.

One minute, John was there; the next, he was gone. Just like that, after 17 years, he walked out. We were at a final fork in the road. I blamed myself for making poor decisions. In retrospect, I shouldn't have taken all the blame; the bitterness rotted my mind and made me feel worthless as a human being.

I was yet to learn another important lesson: *when damaged people commit unnatural acts, they become dangerous to themselves.*

26.
OVERDOSING

"Imagine a society that subjects people to conditions that makes them so unhappy, they need drugs to take away their unhappiness"

— Theodore Kaczynski

2018…

When our heart and mind shatter, normal logic disappears; regrettably, we do "silly things."

After John left, I felt lost somewhere in the universe. Friends didn't recognize me. The truth is I was a useless pile of rubble with no direction or purpose.

Despite my inner demons, I still wanted to be a good mum, so I painted a smile on my face. The day John left, I drove six hours to Peterborough for our daughter's national cheerleading competition. John went to Matthew's football.

As tough as it was, I held it together. Five days later, I held my head up high, packed a suitcase, and headed to the Dublin Writer's Conference to focus on my future—as an author.

I wanted to learn more about the craft of writing fiction and who better to learn from than other authors from across all continents. The conference reinforced my love of writing. It also provided a rare opportunity—pitching a novel for a movie adaption to a Hollywood producer.

I reviewed and revised my pitch, rehearsed, and rehearsed, not knowing how to pitch professionally. Nerves got the better of me. I fell apart at the microphone. I wasn't strong enough; it wasn't my time. Yet, the producer still saw something in me and requested a film treatment. Due to my stumble, I believe that the chance of a new life was ruined. I'd let myself and the kids down. I felt a failure and flew home knowing that I'd probably messed up my one shot.

A week after returning from Dublin, I cooked a BBQ at home and invited John, who declined. I then saw on my Facebook newsfeed he had been out with mutual friends, including Veronica and Ryan, the duo who were the final nail in our coffin.

It destroyed me. Why would John continue to socialize with a man who wanted to bed his wife behind his back? It was twisted. I was enraged. John was partying as though our marriage meant nothing and it hurt more so because he was with the deadly duo. It became clear; the heartstrings connecting John and I had severed forever.

Whatever part of me that was left was obliterated by John's actions. I walked upstairs and told the kids, "I'll always love you." It was my way of saying goodbye. No one cared about me. That was my truth. Vicki was gone. I couldn't take life anymore. My seams were frayed; I had become completely unhinged. My soul was shattered.

I grabbed the medicine box, filled with a variety of solutions for pain: Paracetamol, Codeine, Zapain, Diclofenac, among others. I popped pill after pill as though I were eating Smarties and washed them down with a bottle of rose wine. I dragged my exhausted body outside and collapsed on the garden sofa.

In total darkness, the pills in my quivering palm glowed bright, mirroring the full moon overhead. My mind was full of angry thoughts; my body consumed with bitter resentment. Any dwindling energy I possessed faded to the background. I could not take the pain anymore; my fragile heart was shattered and a collection of unfixable shards. Enough was enough; it was time to depart this woeful life.

I cried hysterically as I tossed the pills down my throat, gulping wine to make them sink quicker and act faster. I just wanted everything to be over. I wanted my head to stop hammering my brain. It hurt, felt like my head was clamped and crushed in a vice.

Surrounded by eerie shadows, unsure of how many tablets I'd consumed, I became terrified, the realization that my death was moments away. I rubbed my sweating palms as erratic heartbeats thumped against my chest. I closed my eyes, waiting for my heart to stop and everything to be over.

I texted John to tell him I'd taken a drug overdose. I begged him to get the kids so that they wouldn't find me. He ignored me, so I ate more pills. At that point, I believed John did not care if I was dead. If he did, he would have had the decency to pick up his phone.

~

Ironically, my friends, Mary and Tina, had been trying to contact me. When Mary didn't receive one of my usual prompt replies, she had a feeling something was wrong. So did Tina, a school friend, who dashed over to my house. Their actions saved my life.

The following minutes were all a blur. Tina arrived with her boyfriend. "Vicki, you silly girl, why didn't you call me?" A paramedic followed, asking me what I'd taken. I handed over the empty blister packets of Paracetamol, Codeine, Zapain and Diclofenac.

Dazed, I sat while he took my blood pressure. It was high - 180/90.

Tina assured me she'd care for the kids until she could get in touch with my sister. I was led into the ambulance and taken to Southmead Hospital in Bristol. The paramedic started talking to me. I didn't retain a word. I realize now he was just trying to keep this lost, afraid girl conscious.

~

I'm not sure when we arrived. It must have been late. There wasn't a soul in the emergency room. I remember seeing a lone black cat outside the emergency doors. Its two dark eyes followed me as I walked on trembling legs. Was it an angel in disguise?

Lights stung my eyes as the paramedic escorted me, arm in arm, to a bright ward. I was placed in a small cubicle. Emotionally spent, I collapsed into a tiny blue leather chair with a hardback. There I sat sobbing and wilting like a dying plant.

Frantic itching, that's a vivid memory. Codeine was causing it. I wanted it to stop. I felt infested with fleas or scabies. I believed I was an annoyance to the nursing staff. Why should the doctors bother to save someone who'd done this to herself? They took bloods to see how bad the damage was and hooked me up to an IV. As I was nursed back to reality, my mind began to clear. I was terrified. What had I done? All I knew at that point was that I no longer wanted to die.

I was filled with shame. It felt as though my soul had been lured into the garden by an evil spirit, but I fought back and escaped. My mind was now filled with joyous images of the two people I loved more than anything in this world—my precious children, Emily and Matthew.

The normal Vicki would have never contemplated abandoning them. I desperately wanted to see them grow up. I felt remorseful and disgusted by my stupid, selfish actions. I was also filled with self-doubt: would my children ever forgive or understand their broken mum?

~

I wept until I was empty. All my energy was gone. It was cold, and I felt uncomfortable listening to painful howls through the paper-thin curtain. I deserved to feel pain, but I was numb with shock and fear.

My sister Shelly arrived at some point. John followed. I couldn't even look at him or let him close. Neither of them knew what to say; they were in shock.

John spoke first. "My friends took my phone, and I never saw your messages." I didn't know if that was the truth. John explained his absence so matter of factly, so unemotional; it said much without saying much. He was in complete denial about his role in pushing me over the edge. I could see in his face he was sick and tired of me—he was emotionally exhausted.

A doctor then came with the blood results and crouched at my feet. I stared at his unsympathetic face. "There's a chance you'll die. Your levels are extremely high." He was referring to acetaminophen poisoning from excessive paracetamol consumption.

"We will try and reverse the damage, but there's no guarantee."

I'll never forget his straight face, just telling me so calmly that I would probably die. He didn't care because I'd done it to myself.

"I'd probably die." Those words resounded in my head. John just stared at the floor. I couldn't even look at Shelly. I just wanted my parents, but they were in Greece. I yearned for them to hug me and tell me that everything was going to be okay. The truth was painfully obvious; assuming I recovered, my life would never be the same again.

I accepted the doctor's prognosis. I didn't cry on the surface. I put on a brave face. Inside, I was drowning in waves of despair and fear. By this stage, I was expectorating with a vengeance. John and my sister emptied my rose wine sick bowls. They were kind.

Hours later, at 5 am, I started my second antidote, a 10-hour Acetylcysteine infusion that would slowly fuel my system. Then I had to wait hours to take more bloods to see if I was, in fact, going to die. It was like being a prisoner on death row, awaiting execution.

I wished I could turn back the clock. I wished that I'd done so many things differently and had never hurt John. I didn't want life to end like that. It was not how I wanted to be remembered.

I wondered as I sat hospitalized, if life was predestined? Was I supposed to go through this to end up where I was meant to be?

~

John and my sister left. There was nothing anyone could do other than wait for the hours and minutes to pass and see if the antidote was having any reverse impact. Shelly needed to get back to her kids, and John wanted to get the school uniforms ready. I don't know if he cared whether I lived or died.

I watched the clock slowly tick. A creepy stranger, sat opposite, stared, x-raying me with his eyes. Disgusted by his perverted ogling, I shut myself behind the curtain. A mental health worker then escorted me to an interview suite. She wanted to know what had led me to such a turning point.

I told her everything, how I'd broken our marriage, and how Veronica, my close friend, had been the final straw making such a vile, untrue accusation, which ultimately destroyed what was left of John and me.

The counselor was kind. I felt as though I was describing an episode of Jeremy Kyle (British tabloid talk show). I wasn't; it was my own miserable life. I think she needed to be sure I wouldn't do it again if I survived and was discharged. I told her I'd made a terrible mistake. She stared; I could see the disbelief in her eyes. I think you would benefit from some professional counseling," she volunteered. I agreed. She gave me an assistance number for Positive Steps.

~

The doctor arrived around 3 pm. "I'm happy to report, the worse is over, you will live." I felt a surge of relief. I would recover! I just wanted to go home and see my children again. I was discharged at 5 pm and came home emotionally and physically drained. John made me a cup of tea, then informed me he was going to London to get ready for a meeting the following day.

Within half an hour, he left me to look after both kids. Unbelievable! Just an hour or two after being discharged, he just left us, expected me to be mum again.

27.
SHELLY HAS MY BACK

"A sister is more than family. She is someone you can call when things aren't going right. She is a forever friend."
— Anonymous

2018…

The doorbell rang. I wasn't expecting anyone.

I felt hopeful. Had John had a change of heart? Did he want to be by my side for support? I slowly dragged my drug-weakened body toward the door, the doorknob jiggled and jiggled. The jiggling felt like someone banging a drum inside my head. Had John forgotten his key?

I looked through the glass panels. It was my sister Shelly. My heart sank. Nothing had changed; John was never coming back. I felt sorry for myself; I had no interest in talking to anyone.

Shelly kept jiggling the door and signaled to open.

"Go away, I'm fine. I don't need your help," I cried, the tears rolling down my cheeks.

What an awful thing for me to say to your own sister. She took it on the chin, remained calm, and smiled, "Open up. I need a cup of coffee."

Shelly won the battle of wits. I opened the door, then walked silently into the kitchen and turned on the kettle.

She stared at my pathetic frail body. "Have you eaten?"

"I'm not hungry," I blurted.

"Look at you; you're skinny as a rake. You must be starving." She went into the cupboard and took out some cookies and made some toast smothered with butter and Marmite (British food spread made from yeast). The sun shone through the window as I carried the tea and coffee into the garden. She followed with the snacks. I had been numb for so many days; I had forgotten what food tasted like.

We sat on the rattan sofa; my tears began to flow. "May I make a suggestion as your older sister?" asked Shelly calmly. I nodded. "I think it's time to move forward; the past is the past. We all experience disappointments. Sometimes, life just happens. Never forget, you have a family that loves you."

It was our first ever heart to heart conversation. The more Shelly talked, the more I realized my attempted overdose was a selfish cry for recognition. I also realized Shelly was more than a sister; she was a *true* friend, unlike so many of the others I *thought* were friends.

~

As we chatted, my mind recalled a cold winter evening when I was about 18. I had been out clubbing in a light dress and high heels when a bit of snow began to fall. (In England, we panic when one inch of snow falls).

The evening was coming to a close, so I decided to head home. To my surprise, the streets were dead silent; all the buses and taxis had been canceled. I had no choice but to walk the four miles home. The walk took about 90 minutes. By the time I stumbled through the door, my legs were numb and turning blue. I was almost frozen. Fortunately, Mum and Dad were fast asleep. Shelly wrapped me up and rubbed my legs until I got the feeling back in them. As she tucked me under the covers, she promised she wouldn't say a thing to Mum or Dad. She has kept that promise to this day.

~

As we sat in that sunny garden, I suddenly realized that, no matter how I messed up my life and how many times I pushed her away, Shelly never gave up on me, like my other so-called friends—Lara, Veronica, and Anna—all of whom who I faithfully supported during their messy separations, domestic abuse issues, and marriages filled with infidelities.

Shelly continued to drink her coffee. "When I left you at the hospital, I was concerned. You looked dreadful," she smiled.

"Charming," I replied. "Do you know how that makes me feel?"

"I didn't say it to hurt your feelings. I said it to make you want to look more like the sister I used to have," said Shelly.

I looked in the mirror. Shelley was right. I no longer vaguely resembled the old fun-loving Vicki. I wondered where the hell she went and if she was ever coming back.

"Don't be mad, but I've made you an appointment to see your doctor this morning.," announced Shelly. "That's in an hour. I'll drive and stay with you."

I shook my head violently.

"I'm just trying to help," she insisted.

"I know you are, but the doctor is going to prescribe antidepressants," I replied.

"Those damn things will make me feel dreadful for weeks before they even begin to kick in. I can't go there; I'll have the urge to kill myself again. And I'm not sure…" I began to sob.

Shelley looked at the dark rings around my eyes and cradled her arms around me. "Okay, no doctors."

"No pills, just sausages," I said. Shelly smiled. For some reason, I remembered Shelly cradling Matthew in her arms at my hospital bed, admiring him. She loved her perfect little nephew and for some funny reason nicknamed him "sausages." The nickname stuck.

As I thought back over the years, Shelly always had my back. When I was recovering from my back operation, she would stop by to see if I needed any help with anything.

On the surface, we have little in common, other than our hazel eyes and streak of tenderness. Shelly has a head of thick dark hair, is self-confident, vigorously practical, and owns a mischievous sense of humor. Over the years, she drove Nan and Gramps mad by removing lightbulbs, changing their clocks, put a

For Sale sign outside their house. She also bubble wrapped my car and added a big red bow. I knew better than to retaliate; she'd always go one better!

My hair is lighter and thinner than Shelly's. She's an extrovert, whereas I, tend to be insecure despite my cheery exterior. I also don't take rejection well, and I have a strong desire to accomplish something significant professionally.

Shelly's unwavering support also taught me a most important life lesson: *No matter what life throws at us, what shit we get ourselves in, those who really love you will always be there offering support.*

28.
RUNNING AND RUNNING

"The only way to escape fear is to run toward it. The more difficult the victory; the greater the happiness."

— Kenny Nola

2018…

After a botched attempt at overdosing, it was difficult playing the happy, carefree mum.

Talk about crazy! Although John didn't want anything to do with me, I still wanted my prince back. I missed us being a family. His traveling left me unlimited time to conjure the worst. Was I the sole cause of John leaving? Did he, too, have some dark secrets?

Then there were my parents. I was convinced they loved John more than me. He was the respectful father; I was the mum acting out of character. They seemed to forget I was the full-time parent—I'd brought our children up 80 per cent of the time while he galavanted across the country.

I sensed I was slipping down the slippery slope to depression hell. This time, I decided to seek professional help and completed a wellness telephone interview with health professionals. Unfortunately, I was told there was a "three-month wait" before I could enroll on any course. Disgraceful!

So, I decided I would take each day as it came and make myself better and give my Matthew and Emily the mum they deserved.

~

I began my self-recovery plan with a call to John. In retrospect, it was probably not the smartest thing. I left a voicemail apologizing for tearing us apart. A day later, I left another voicemail. I told him I missed *us* and that his support would get me out of my state of depression. I even asked if he would consider couples counselling and therapy. Again, nothing, but I still wasn't ready to throw in the towel.

One evening, feeling lost and alone, I began to look at the pictures of our memories. We were the model family that lost its way. I decided to express my true feelings in a photo slideshow, featuring our 17 years together with Haim's "Want You Back" as the soundtrack.

> Some things are long forgotten
> Some things were never said
> We were on one endless road
> But I had a wandering heart…
> …I'll take the fall and the fault in us
> I'll give you all the love I never gave before I left you
> Just know that I want you back

© *Haim. I want you back.*

I thought the emotion of the video would move him. It took me six hours to make and crashed three times, but I never gave up. I cried myself to sleep watching the video after sending a copy to John.

He replied the next day. "That video made me cry. It was a lovely thing to do. Those memories are there and should never be forgotten."

I took his response as a glimmer of hope. He also agreed to set off for Blackpool at 7 am to attend Emily's cheer competition, *as a family*. Afterward, we enjoyed the rides at Blackpool Pleasure Beach. The rides recalled my deliriously happy childhood days with Mum, Dad, Nan, Gramps, and Shelly.

~

A few days later, John and I had the most honest and painful conversation ever. I apologized and told him I still loved him.

His response was like a dagger in my heart. "Vicki, I'm lonely and stressed too, but I don't think I have the answers you want. I'm not sure *us* could ever work again."

I attempted to keep the dialogue going with a text, "I'm truly lost and lonely without you." Again, no reply. I was crushed by John's silence.

The next day Matthew injured himself. It was a serious injury to his hip, requiring crutches for the entire summer. I took care of him and at the same time, I decorated Emily's room with a cheerleading theme (cheer bows, pictures, and flags). I wanted it to be special for when she was home—Matt already had a Southampton FC room.

John texted to let me know he planned a football tournament while Matthew was still on crutches. I thought his intention was inappropriate. "Surely, you are joking!" I was only interested in Matthew's welfare—the doctor had strictly ordered rest.

John snapped. "Do you do anything but complain? It's the same length training would have been."

"He isn't even meant to train! I'm only interested in Matthew resting," I said. "I don't want him to end up with a hip pin."

"It's my business what I do on my weekends with the kids," replied John in a raised voice, "not yours!"

I fell, quick and hard. He didn't seem to care about worsening Matthew's injury. Football came first again, above his own son's health! The argument broke me into pieces and I quickly spiraled back into the dark abyss. It was like an invisible magnet, pulling me under.

~

Not long after the row, Mary called. She sensed I wasn't in a good place again. She said I seemed down, insisted we met and assured me that I was stronger than I thought.

As we sat and talked, Mary listened attentively. I told her about the row and said that being alone in the house without the kids was depressing. "Let me be there for you," begged Mary. "It's okay to feel down, but don't allow the disappointment to become unbearable. Please let your loved ones in."

After the call ended, John and I had two more bitter text conversations. Looking back, I sounded like a crazy lady.

"Do you know how close I am to ending my life? The last memory you'll have of us is rowing because you raised your voice at me!"

"It's time for you to stop piling crap like that on me. You're the one who's not being fair!"

"I'm just telling you how I feel. My death would be an inconvenience to you because you'd have to take care of the kids full time."

"Christ, why do you keep saying stuff like that?"

"Football was a major part of what went wrong between us."

"Do you know how crazy that sounds?"

"We never did anything as a four, we always split up. Carry on telling me I'm crazy, and I'll do it again, only next time, I'll end it."

"Stop. Stop. No more."

"I'm trying to tell you what went wrong in our marriage. All I've ever wanted to do was renew our wedding vows."

There was no reply.

A few days later, John acted as if the prior conversation never took place. "I have work issues; could we swap days with the kids?"

"I may not be here much longer. I love my children, but you can look after them, give them everything they need. No one needs me. I'm a waste of space."

"We can both look after them. You're not a waste of space. Stop beating yourself up."

"You keep the kids. I don't deserve them. I'm ready to go now."

"Stop doing this."

"You are so cold. You may as well stab the knife in me."

"Why the hell would you message me that?"

"Because I'm going for good. Goodbye." I meant it.

~

I grabbed my Converse trainers and bolted out of the house, gasping for air. I ran and ran into the fields of Wick St Lawrence. I suppose, I thought I was escaping my life by running away. Exhausted, some two or three kilometers later, I lay shivering in a field and cried.

My eyes closed. I've no idea how long for. I decided to text John. "You did this to me. I cannot go on." I ended the text with what most people would consider an irrational request. "Publish my book; that's all I ask. It's on my laptop." That may sound trite but publishing the *Kill List* novel was all I ever wanted. It would demonstrate I could succeed as a professional author and the kids would be proud.

John replied immediately. "Where are you?" He never mentioned my last request. It must have seemed frivolous, irrelevant, or that I was completely out of my mind.

~

I was now certain. Nobody cared. That was my twisted *truth*. Hurt flooded my brain. *No more!* I just wanted it to stop. I felt a complete failure and believed it would be impossible to fix my life.

Confused and upset, I dragged my weary feet another mile or so. I found myself at the motorway bridge. My body was robotic, my mind swirling—the two were not connected. All logic was gone.

As I came to a stop on the bridge, the heavens opened. The rain saturated my hair and rolled down my cheeks. My clothes were completely waterlogged; every inch of me was numb and freezing. I was a body without a soul. I wrapped my raw red fingers around the grey metal railings and pulled myself onto the rough surface. I slipped and needed to pull myself up a second time.

Trembling and balling my eyes out, I finally had my legs hovering on both sides of the railing. There was nobody to stop me. The drop below was a good 30 feet. I lifted my left leg over the rail and sat on top, watching rows of cars whoosh past. The wind felt like a centrifugal force pulling my legs downward. If I jumped, there would be no doubt, I'd splatter all over the highway.

I wailed hysterically, drowning the sound of the cars. I loosened my grip on the railing and leaned forward. I became lightheaded; my heart pounded erratically, I felt a massive pain in my chest and arms; I assumed I was having a massive heart attack.

Without warning, my head experienced a sharp pop, as though I'd crashed through an invisible hypnotic barrier. Suddenly, I was in the present and out of a trance. I looked down at the speeding cars and felt terrified. If I died here and now, it would complicate my children's lives forever, what would they tell their children about their Grandmother? Suppose I fell on a car filled with innocent children and they died?

I started to climb off the railing, I slipped and held on for dear life. Somehow, I pulled myself up, got back on my feet and walked away from death.

John had alerted the police that I was a missing person. Next thing I knew, a grey-haired officer pulled up in one of the country lanes.

"Young lady, have you been on the motorway bridge?" he asked sternly.

Stupidly I answered, "Yes, I stopped briefly, but I'm on my way home now."

"Is that right," he said.

I nodded my head like a bobblehead doll.

"Come and sit in my car," he said. "Let's talk."

I did as I was told. Once inside, he informed me that if I got back out, he'd detain me under the Mental Health Act. I was a danger to myself and others. That shocked me.

The officer radioed ahead to say he'd found me. He handed me the phone. "Someone wants to talk to you."

"Vicki, where the hell are you?" John said.

"In a police car."

"I know, they've been round here. I didn't call them, your mum did."

"Clearly, you weren't that concerned."

"I've been driving around looking for you for two hours."

"Don't waste your time."

"Stop putting everyone through this."

"Don't you realize I'm here because you're so horrible to me."

The officer sat and listened. "You stay right here," he said sternly. He got out of the car, made a call, then returned. "Listen, if you agree to being dropped to a friend or a family member, you're free to go."

~

We drove to my friend Nadia's house, who lived just minutes from me. I hated the fact that the neighbors saw me getting out a police car. I didn't want to embarrass myself or her. She didn't care; she embraced me and called me a silly girl.

The policeman left when a male mental health worker came to assess me. "Young lady," he said, "I think you'd benefit from professional counseling."

"I agree," I replied. "But I've been told there's a three-month wait." He shrugged his shoulders as though it was normal.

I laid my cards on the table, told him everything I'd been through, and that I wanted to go home. He then walked into the kitchen and relayed our entire conversation to Nadia and her husband!

I flew off the handle, told him I had fully cooperated, and he had no right to share my personal life. He didn't like my reply. "Let's sit down and talk a bit more," he said.

I was done with talking now that he'd broken my confidence. I ran out the door to a nearby friend, Andy, crouched on his doorstep, so nobody could see me, and knocked. He opened the door, flabbergasted.

"Please just let me in, and I'll explain everything," I begged.

Andy nodded. I told him everything. He assured me I was safe.

~

Eventually, I snuck home. Bad move! The cops were waiting. I tried to run again but bumped into Nadia. "Vicki, stop running, you're only making matters worse for yourself."

"I'm tired. I need to sleep. I just want to be left alone," I screeched.

Eventually, the police agreed to leave on the condition I would call Nadia when I woke.

"Don't let us down," he said.

~

My sister Shelly arrived and told me my parents were coming over.

Boy, was I mad. "Leave me alone. I just want to sleep and forget everything."

Mum and Dad appeared and shouted. "You've worried us sick. We've been looking everywhere for you!"

The shouting wasn't helping. The last thing I needed was a lecture.

"If you don't stop yelling, I'll jump out of the window. I mean it." Mum shouted at Dad, "Just leave her." I was exhausted and alone. I hid under the duvet cover in the dark.

I texted John. "I know I've been horrible to you, but I need kind words; no shouting."

John replied matter of factly, "Vicki, I'm not shouting. Get some sleep. Tomorrow's another day."

~

I had a dreadful night's sleep. I realized that I desperately needed a helping hand. Exercise alone was cutting it. I decided to pay £60 to see a private therapist, and then decide how to proceed.

The session had an odd dynamic. The therapist sat listening; she didn't take notes and rarely spoke. While it was good to get things off my chest, I felt humiliated by sharing all my problems. It also felt as though she was content to sit on her backside looking unsympathetic.
She looked at her watch often. I imagined she was calculating her fees.

As for advice at the end of the session, she suggested I write a letter to my mum explaining my feelings, how I'd felt ever since John had left and how the actions of others had made me feel.

I figured I had nothing to lose. The letter took me four hours to write. I cried the whole time and then put it in Mum's letterbox. She said the letter was like reading one of my novels. I felt completely misunderstood, and that the therapy session had been a complete waste of my time and £60. I would not go back. There was no point! The only person that could help me was myself. I would have to keep on fighting for life and keep putting one foot in front of the other until I found myself back on the right path.

29.
GIVE MUMMY A BIG HUG

"A mother's arms are more comforting than anyone else's."
— Diana, Princess of Wales

2018…

When you're lost and lonely, you just want a big hug and to be told everything would be okay.

After multiple suicide attempts and my bitterness and resentment towards John and my ex-friends, I realized everyone felt sorry for John. No one had any sympathy for broken me. Why would they? Most people thought I was to blame for the marriage breakup: I'd sinned, and I got what I deserved. If I were in their shoes, I probably would have felt the same way.

But I choose to keep my personal affairs behind closed doors. No one knew how miserable I was. That I was tackling grief, anxiety, depression, the early loss of loved one, a cancer scare, and major back surgery, all while working full time and bringing up two kids, pretty much alone.

There are other aspects I don't wish to share to avoid embarrassing John—I'm not that wicked. Suffice to say, there are two sides to every story. But it was important to my ego and my pride that I maintained the appearance of a perfect life. My Facebook world was filled with pictures and posts of lavish holidays and the happy moments—no one posts that they are miserable, depressed, and want to kill themselves, do they?

I tried to act like the old Vicki. I didn't want people to think I was completely mad. But I did imagine people were whispering behind my back and believed they were enjoying my downfall, some more than others.

In a moment of utter despair, I confided in my friend Nadia. I told her the whole truth, perhaps for the first time in my life. "Why didn't you confide in me earlier?" she asked.

"I don't know, I guess I was embarrassed and didn't want to admit that my life wasn't perfect."

"I've helped friends in the past and it's backfired, so now I give people distance, unless they ask for help," Nadia admitted.

Truth was I didn't want to reveal details of my private life. Or ask for help. I've since discovered those with mental health issues don't ask for help. They sit alone and suffer in silence.

Nadia continued. "I'm not surprised people are ignoring your pain. You're a master at putting on a smiley mask."

She was right. No one realized that behind my smile was a sad woman who had felt rejected for years. I yearned for a big Mummy and Daddy hug, but I was too embarrassed to ask, given my mistakes. I knew my parents blamed me for pushing John away.

A surprised Nadia replied, 'I don't understand."

"It's complicated. My parents adore John. He's the father of their grandchildren, so they see no reason to abandon him. They have conveniently forgotten the times I was left a football widow or alone with the children for days on end."

"They probably want to maintain some kind of normality for the kid's sake," said Nadia.

I didn't care to respond, I wanted sympathy. "I also find it difficult when it's John's weekend with the kids. My parents go out of their way to cook a roast dinner and invite everyone but me. I felt isolated, as though John had stolen my parents from me. I'd sit home staring at the four walls for hours imagining my sister, her husband and their two kids, Nan, John, Emily, and Matthew cozily sitting around the dining table smiling, laughing, enjoying a good home-cooked meal. The stress and anxiety stole my appetite. I couldn't bring myself to eat for weeks, lost 40 pounds, and looked like a ghost."

There is not a day that goes by that I don't wonder why my parents insist on maintaining good relations with John. At first, I thought they wanted us to get back together. My parent's life has been good; they've been married for decades suffering little tragedy—aside from agonizing parental deaths. But deep down, I realize they want to keep John on their side for fear of seeing their grandchildren less. I finally understand.

Then there's me. I'd always been the responsible, educated daughter with a highflying career and the appetite for a wealthy lifestyle. They simply didn't know how to deal with this same person suddenly in crisis.

~

John's parents, Sarah and Peter, are an entirely different matter. After my hospitalization, they never called or sent a text. They never reached out even once to check on my welfare.

I was their daughter-in-law for 17 years, but they never showed any compassion for my battle with my demons. Rather they have gone out of their way to make me feel worthless.

When I was strong enough, I messaged them and told them how they'd made me feel. Hoping for a different response, I suggested, "Perhaps it was best if we had no contact." Sarah responded curtly and dispassionately, "Sorry, you feel that way." The response left me thinking, imagining what they said to John behind my back? Did they have a hand in poisoning our well? I'll never know that answer, and they are not about to volunteer their true feelings.

I now realize that *unless someone experiences torment and depression first-hand, it is hard to imagine, difficult to articulate, and almost impossible to treat with drugs and counseling alone.*

~

I cry as I write these passages because my mum and dad mean the world to me, my entire family does, and knowing that I dragged them through hell is distressing. One day, I hope they will forgive me. I pray that they will understand during the terrible times, I was not the Vicki they once loved and cherished.

I hope they will also understand that I'm sharing my story because I want to inspire other people in difficult times, encourage them to keep fighting for life because it's precious. We only get one life, and that life is too short. I also hope that Mum and Dad will help nurture the old Vicki back to life. I want them to be proud of me, and I want to build many more wonderful memories with them.

Mum and Dad, I apologize to you for everything. I will love you until the day I die. I only ask one thing: "Please give me a *big hug* when you see me. Tell me I'm not a disappointment."

30.
KATHERINE GOES AWOL

"Don't feel sad over someone who gave up on you, feel sorry for them because they gave up on someone who would have never given up on them."

— Frank Ocean

2018…

Godfather Michael Corleone said, "Keep your friends close, and your enemies closer." Sometimes, I find it hard to decide who's who.

Twenty-seven years. That's how long Katherine and I had been best friends. We'd been through everything together.

We'd been attached at the hip since age 11 when we met in primary school. We shared all our secrets, and I always had her back.

Katherine and I were known as the dancing queens. "Come on, Vickster, let's strut some moves," she'd always say, offering a beaming smile and a cheeky wink. We were disco divas on the dance floor. "We'll still have fun when we are old and grey and sneak out of our nursing homes to go clubbing," she'd tease.

I made Katherine my bridesmaid and Emily's Godmother. I loved her as though she were part of my own family. I truly believed she would be a permanent fixture in my life.

For eight years, I was her support system, her cheerleader, her rock, while she struggled to get a visa to bring her husband, Dan, and two children, Olivia and Elsie, home from Australia. Their visas kept being declined. Katherine faced an expensive ongoing battle to win the right to return to her OWN country with her family. It was unfair.

"You know that I'll do whatever I can to help you," I promised. I even contacted our local Member of Parliament to see if there was anything he could do to assist.

Eventually, thousands of dollars later and an eight-year stint overseas away from family and friends at home, visas were granted.

"I'm coming home," she screeched excitedly. I'd felt as though I'd never hear those words and just cried.

During her absence, I'd Skype, write letters, send parcels with English goodies that she missed, birthday gifts for her and the kids. Anything I could think of to keep her spirits high. I would have climbed mountains for her or crossed oceans. I was also only one of two friends who bothered to fly to the other side of the world to attend her wedding. Katherine was overwhelmed.

I'd also visited her former school, and made a special DVD filled with personal messages from all the kids in her class, and apologies and congratulations from all her friends who could not attend her big day.

When Katherine did come home, I welcomed her with open arms, invited her into my friendship circle, and included her family at social gatherings. I tried my best to make it an easy transition.

I'd even nurtured her when she suspected her husband of cheating. She'd found train tickets and dinner-for-two receipts and confronted him. His betrayal was clear. He'd even hid the damning evidence.

"I'm sure it's nothing, but you do need to talk to him. If it's innocent, why did he hide the receipts and bank statements from you?"

Teary-eyed, Katharine shrugged. She just wanted to forget about it and pretend their marriage was okay. "Isn't that what we do, just plod on?" She said, then confessed they were not happy. She'd cook dinner, and he wouldn't join the family at the table, choosing to stay upstairs.

Dan had admitted that his work trip away was with a female colleague but stated nothing had happened. I still wondered, why hide all the receipts? Guilty conscience? Perhaps. It was none of my business. I'd only be there if she needed a shoulder to cry on.

I believe Katherine didn't want to accept he lied or become a single Mum with three kids. It's a fact that both men and women are capable of cheating on their partners. One day, some version of the truth will emerge. I would have been there offering support when it did, but regrettably, we are no longer friends.

~

Things changed as soon as Katherine landed in the UK and unexpectedly fell pregnant. It was tough, she and Dan were living at her parent's house and neither of them had jobs, so trying to rent a home was tough. We even let them move into our house for two weeks while we went on holiday!

Dan eventually found a job. After learning of the pregnancy, Katherine chose not to socialize, which is understandable. I was busy too, taking care of my kids and running my PR firm, and busy working on my crime novel. Time just seemed to fly by, that's life!

Katherine gave birth to a boy, Oliver. I couldn't wait to meet him. But for some reason, she didn't want to invite me over. She later admitted she was embarrassed that her rented house was small. That was silly, I couldn't care. I thought our friendship was deeper than that. I would have been satisfied eating a pizza sitting on the floor, playing with the baby, and watching a movie.

Life was hard, with a new-born and two young girls. I get that. I frequently offered to help. But she was always busy mixing with other toddler mums. I did attend her baby shower and bought gifts. I also always bought all three children birthday and Christmas presents and included them at my own children's birthdays. John and I would invite them over for meals and we did get invited over a couple times to their new, bigger house in the country for birthday parties.

~

Out of the blue, the dynamics changed between us. She was no longer the fun-loving girl I once knew. She became cold and distant. I wonder if I did something to upset her, but there was no row, no crossed words. I can say hand on heart I do not know why her behavior changed. I think during my messy separation, I may have unintentionally missed one of their daughter's birthdays. Maybe she was annoyed that I didn't help organize her baby shower, but I didn't wish to interfere with her sister's arrangements.

Reading this, you must be thinking, come on, spill the beans. Surely something happened to make us drift. I must have done something for the friendship to dissolve. I've had the same thoughts, pondered over and over, and over again, trying to figure out what I did wrong, but I cannot find a reason.

I wish there were a blaring row because at least I'd know the answer; why she was the third Domino to fall. I feel utter sadness and devastation. It's as though Katherine set up a new home, in a new village, and no longer wanted me as a fixture in her new life.

~

The distance between us seemed to get worse when there was no John. After we separated, I wanted all the moral support I could gather. But I never received a single phone call or text from Katherine. As my life tumbled into the abyss, the suicides, the overdose, Katherine remained silent, as if I didn't exist. Ironically, her husband Dan helped John to move into his new place, took him out for beers, and the occasional meal. Her strange behavior cut deeply.

Three months after John left, Katherine finally called to check on me. Was her life that busy? The call made me bitter and resentful. After everything I'd done for her over the years, my oldest friend was not there when I needed her the most. Perhaps some kindnesses at that point would have helped me avoid the motorway bridge incident. Admittedly, I should have reached out and asked for her help, but I struggling with what I now realized was my own mental illness.

~

As you read what I have written, it must be obvious—I'm not the person who copes well with upset. My complaints may seem trite, even bitchy, but I felt let down by the one person who meant the world to me. But when I get deeply depressed, I become mired at the bottom of a cavernous black hole in my psyche. I can barely get from one day to the next. Some days, I remember little or nothing.

Nevertheless, the bottom line was I was battling severe depression, and I needed her to be there for me. Maybe she didn't agree with my choices. Yes, I'd made stupid, regrettable mistakes, but that's life. People screw up. If the shoe had been on the other foot, I'd have been there for her. I'd have gone to her house and let her cry on my shoulder.

Weeks later, she called a second time. I was brutally blunt. I told her after twenty years of laughter, fun, weddings, and babies; she didn't care about me anymore. It told her that her behavior hurt as much, if not more, than my separation from John. Then I hung up.

As the weeks rolled by, I made a new year's resolution to repair the damage I left in my wake. I messaged Katherine in January 2019, apologizing for being brutally honest. I tried to explain that I wasn't myself and that I had even made three suicide attempts.

All she could say was, "Vicki, we have chosen different directions, as people sometimes do. I'm sure your lovely children and family get you through the worst times. And, I do hope you get the professional support you need."

She did add some kind words: "If you need me, you know where I am. Life is short and every second precious, so look to those that mean the most to you. No one can predict what's around the corner."

Her response felt phony. I was convinced she didn't mean a word she said. I wondered when I died if she'll even attend my funeral. The reality is, *no matter how long you've known someone, how much you adore them, the only person that has your back is you! Unless you have a sister named Shelly.*

31.

ONE FOR THE TEAM

**"Let us sacrifice our today
so that our children can have a better tomorrow."**
— A.P.J Abdul Kalam

2018…

Watching my son take off and land in a professional flight simulator at the age of 13 was pretty cool!

Our 16th wedding anniversary arrived. I gave John a 'Thinking of You' card. I didn't want the milestone to pass without acknowledging all the good years. It was my way of showing some affection, but my pleas fell on deaf ears.

Our arms-length separation continued. We took good care of the kids and ignored each other. Matthew, now 13, was still on crutches from the football injury, and I felt dreadful that he could not play out like all of his friends during the summer holiday.

After browsing the internet, I came up with a cool idea. I'd book him time and lessons on a professional flight simulator at a flying club. Matthew had talked of being a pilot when he grew up; the flight simulator experience would give him a taste of future possibilities. I made the call to book a reservation. "Sorry, madam," said the voice on the other end. "We currently have an eight-week waiting list." I was disappointed for him and me. More rejection—nothing I did ever seemed to work out.

~

A few hours later, I received a message from the flying school: "Give me a call, Robert." It turned out the flying club was owned by my first landlord; I'd done some PR work for him in the past. "If you like," he said, "I can squeeze you in tomorrow at 9 am." Matthew and I set off the flying school with Robert as his instructor.

Once onboard, Matthew soared through the sky as though he'd been flying for years. Even his landings were perfect. "You have a skill for this," declared Robert, who informed me, that under the law, Matthew would be eligible to begin taking solo flying lessons at the age of 14. I told John everything. He was quite supportive of my suggested training plan for our son.

~

Soon, Robert contacted me, saying it was great to see me. He also said he was sorry to learn I'd separated. Then he asked if I'd go out to the movies as friends. I hesitated, but Mum said it was only right since he had been kind enough to squeeze us in on such short notice.

Mum was right, I did owe him, and he'd also promised to let Matthew fly one of his planes as a co-pilot the next time he went to the flying school. I couldn't let that go; it would be a wonderful experience for Matthew.

Even though I craved some male companionship, I wasn't remotely attracted to Robert, who was some ten years older. But most of my supposed friends hadn't bothered to check on me during my emotional roller-coaster, and Katherine, vanished completely. At least, Robert would be company.

He picked me up in his black Porsche. I knew Robert was a businessman, but I didn't realize the extent of his wealth. I was not after his money. Robert set out trying to impress me by booking the Director's Hall, an intimate posh cinema auditorium with a bar. First, we had a drink. We chatted, though I was not interested in his role as a councilor, it bored me—I hated politics.

I was drinking sweet rose wine. I had about half of my drink left when I popped to the toilet. When I returned, it tasted vile. Surely, he couldn't have put anything in my drink.

We chatted, and I tried to finish my wine, all the time thinking this doesn't taste quite right, so I left it. We headed into the theater to watch The Meg, a science fiction movie about a 75-foot Megalodon shark on a huge widescreen. Robert tried to hold my hand. He smiled, "Friends try to comfort friends." His eyes told a different story.

The drive home was fine until he missed the motorway turning. I asked where he was going. He answered, "My place, for a drink!" I'd no choice in the matter and sat quietly as we rolled up to his electric gated mansion. Even in the dark, it was impressive. We entered through the garage, passing more cars and motorbikes.

I was surprised by the interior; the furniture was dated, but I guess he was an older man living alone without a woman's touch. He had three cats; people with animals are kind, aren't they?

The TV was ridiculously huge. He told me to sit down, and he'd get us some wine. I stupidly drank it. Before I knew it, he led me upstairs. I could walk robotically, but my brain had switched off. The next thing I recall was Robert on top of me. I was numb and couldn't speak or fight him off before falling unconscious.

An hour or two later, I awoke with chest pains. There was no doubt in my mind, Robert had spiked me. I crept out his room and fled.

~

I walked down a country road, freezing in the pitch black. I had no idea where I was and called a taxi. I should have called the police but was too afraid and felt ill. The operator told me to keep walking until I came to a road sign. I was scared out of my mind. How could I have been so foolish? Yet, I'd known him for 17 years. I stood in the freezing cold and was eventually picked up by the taxi. A&E (accident and emergency department) was closed so I rang the emergency line 101. The operator asked if I was safe. I said, "I think so."

"Good," she replied. "I would suggest you wait until A&E opens at 8 AM in the morning."

I sat shaking for the next four hours in my bedroom.

~

The following morning, I told the hospital A&E staff, I suspected I'd been drugged and taken advantage of. They asked if I had any proof. Humiliated, I said, the stuff should still be in my bloodstream.

"Madam," replied the doctor, "We can't take any blood work for drug testing. I suggest you go to the police station, make a report and have the blood drawn for analysis." I was too afraid. I didn't want any publicity in the papers. I went home.

Soon, I received a text from Robert asking why I'd left. I told him I knew he'd drugged me. He hit the roof, saying, "How dare you accuse me of such a thing." He protested to the point where I doubted myself. An enormous bouquet of pink and cream roses, lilies, gerbera, and chrysanthemums arrived at the door in a black vase.

Shortly after, I received a text from Robert. He insisted it had all been a horrible mistake. By the time he was finished arguing his case, I felt guilty for making such an accusation. He seized upon my vulnerability and convinced me I was mistaken. *Looking back, I know what really happened that night.*

32.

TAKING SIDES

"Running away from your problems is a race you'll never win."

— Anonymous

2018…

One of the great things about dogs is they love you unconditionally and don't take sides.

Days after, not having told a soul what had happened, I received an email from EasyJet that pissed me off: John had canceled *my* flight to Murcia, Spain. He was taking the kids on *our* annual family holiday without me. How could he not even tell me? I knew if I just stayed home and looked at the four walls, I'd do something silly again.

I decided to run away from life and catch the next plane out of the country to my favorite part of the world—Greece. The first flight I found was leaving for the Greek island of Kefalonia, a place I'd always wanted to visit. Shelly tried to stop me, fearing I might not return. She stole my passport. I demanded it back.

"Where are you going?" she quizzed.

"I'll tell you when I get there."

The last thing I wanted was for someone to book and come with me. I wanted to be alone, far away from my troubled life. I had to make a statement, and told John, "I will not allow you to take the kids away from me and try to destroy me!" I was conflicted. Angry and confident; insecure and dependent.

~

I met a man at the airport bar as I waited for my plane. I bought myself a wine, he bought himself a pint but then we walked to separate tables. It was awkward because we were chatting like old friends, and then headed off in different directions, two tables apart. Johnny then caught my eye. "Shall we sit together; it seems silly that we are both sitting alone!"

"Sure, why not," I answered. "Company would be nice.' I hated being alone.

He was sincere and genuine, unlike Robert. "Shame we're not going to the same country," he said.

Johnny was traveling to Sorrento to clear his head. He had two kids the same age as mine, and he was in the middle of a messy separation. "I've always wanted to go to Sorrento. I thought that it would be a good place to be alone and think."

"So, it's not just me running away from problems," I smiled.

"Everybody has problems," he replied. The only difference is how we handle them."

We friended on Facebook, and he insisted I message him to say I'd arrived safely. On the way up the mountain in the cab, I confirmed my arrival. He replied, "Pleased to hear that you arrived safely. If you don't like it there, you can always catch a plane to Sorrento, and we can hang out."

The further up the mountain we climbed, the darker it became. I was overwhelmed by guilt. I knew my family cared and just wanted me to be safe, so I called home to tell them everything was okay and not to worry. Mum answered the phone. There was an awkwardness in her voice.

"Vicki, it's a bit difficult to talk right now," she whispered.

"Why?" I asked.

"John's here with the kids, and so is Katherine and her husband. We've had a BBQ."

My insides were filled with bitter irony. John was having drinks with my family, in my absence. Mum and Dad were making it abundantly clear—they wanted John in their life. Their strong bonds made me feel like the odd-person-out.

I get that John was their son-in-law for 17 years, but isn't it usually the norm to sever the ties when a marriage breaks down?

I was furious. I'd been out of the country just a few hours, and *my family* and former friends were socializing with John at my parents' house. I yelled at Mum, "Clearly, you've chosen sides. I'm never coming home. You'll never, ever have to see me again."

I meant every word. I was done. Life was carrying on, everyone playing happy families, without me. Looking back, I realize Mum had concluded our family would never be normal. She just wanted to maintain a semblance of order for the sake of the children.

~

I drank two glasses of wine while sitting on the balcony feeling sad and depressed, then woke to a beautiful, sunny island setting. My spirits perked up. There was not a soul in sight. I made my way to the pool and sunbathed alone beneath the mountains. Inexplicably, my creative juices flowed. I thought, what a wonderful setting for a novel. I imagined how easy it would be to dump a body beneath the rocks. It would be an undiscovered final resting place—the unsolved case of a missing tourist.

The pad came out. I scribbled like crazy writing the first two chapters about a woman who had run away from home and wound up murdered. Little did I know the town I was visiting had made the headlines. Some locals informed me a couple had died in a satanic ritual, months earlier.

That night, I'd walked to a fish taverna and bravely dined alone eating red mullet. People stared; they felt sorry for me. I didn't care. As I finished, I received a text from my dog-sitter Shannon. She'd bathed Bella and found some fleas. I'd treated Bella just days earlier at the vet, so I could not understand why she still had them. What did she expect me to do from Greece?

We exchanged heated messages. It seemed I couldn't do anything right. First, the family, now the dog! I replied to

Shannon, "I'm done. I'm going to walk into the sea and disappear."

"Stop it, don't do anything stupid," begged Shannon. "I'm sorry. Don't worry about the dog. Just enjoy your holiday."

I left the taverna and stood on the promenade staring through tears at the black ocean. Those old feelings began to rear their ugly heads. I thought to myself, could I ever be free of the pain and torment? Was my life even worth living?

Suddenly, I regained my mental clarity; the feisty Vicki fought back. I concluded, Matthew and Emily were my children —I would never leave them. Secondly, I was not ready to punch my ticket to hell just yet. Christ, I was still only 37.

I headed back up the mountain to my hotel room. That night I fell into a deep sleep for the first time in months.

~

The next day I continued writing more chapters by the pool using the occasional Greek lager for inspiration. My phone was on fire. Robert kept messaging to check on my whereabouts. He began to woo me with love song after love song. He begged me to fly to the Isle of Jersey with him in one of his planes. I still didn't fancy him, but at that moment, Robert was the only companionship I had. And he was willing to take me under his wing when no one else would.

Two ladies with northern British accents and bikinis arrived at the pool to sunbathe. We got to chatting. I told them how I'd come to be alone there. My phone kept vibrating. I told them about Robert, the millionaire, who wanted me to fly away with him.

"I would go," said one.

"But, he's so much older than me. What will people say?" I responded faintly.

"Who cares what other people think," said the taller woman. "Life is meant for living. Besides, it sounds like he is enamored with you!"

I sat thinking long and hard. John and the family didn't even know if I was still alive. Mum never called me back.

Screw everyone! I did what any scorned woman would do; I accepted my millionaire's invitation. *Big mistake!*

33.

50 SHADES OF ROBERT

"If you lie down with dogs, you get up with fleas."
— **Benjamin Franklin**

2018…

Sometimes, the devil can appear to have a bizarre charm.

I left Greece and flew to Bristol Airport, where my millionaire buddy Robert was waiting for me in arrivals with a funny "Author FitzGerald" sign to embarrass me. The plan was to fly to the Isle of Jersey in the morning in his four-seater plane. I didn't tell Mum and Dad what I was doing; they still didn't even know if I was alive. Soon, they would learn my whereabouts through Facebook. Mum had already protested, "Robert is much too old; Robert has a violent temper, according to rumors." I had told her I was a grown woman who was perfectly capable of making her own decisions. I could feel Mum's eyes roll.

~

The following day Robert and I flew to the Isle of Jersey with two of his friends. He wasn't my hot dream pilot, but as we climbed through the clouds, I felt like Anastasia Steel in *50 Shades of Grey*. I'd decided I'd rather be spoiled rotten than sitting home alone, depressed.

The weather had turned vicious; the plane jostled around at 15,000 feet. I began to perspire, thinking the worst. Robert remained cool and collected. "Turbulence," he said calmly, "Always feels worse than it is." He was quite the accomplished pilot, replotting courses and alternating between manual and automatic modes as he navigated his way through the storm clouds.

"Relax, love, it's all good," he smiled. An hour later, we landed safe and sound. A car picked us up and whisked us to a charming hotel with water views. I stood in the rear of the reservation area, as an annoyed Robert dramatically waved his arms.

"I'm sorry," he said upon returning.

"About what?"

"I been coming here for years," he said. "They know my damn preferences. Somehow the staff mixed up our reservation for the penthouse suite with the hot tub."

I laughed. "Third world problems, hey!"

I enjoyed the company of his hip, mid-sixties friends during what turned out to be a delicious, three-course meal. After dinner, we headed for a crowded local bar with a popular DJ where couples strutted their stuff on the dance floor. It was obvious Jersey was a millionaire's playground; there were dolly birds everywhere trawling for wealthy men. I thought to myself, that's probably how Robert and I look. I didn't care. He was putting a smile on my face. I had almost forgotten what it was like to have a good time.

~

The next evening after dinner, we returned to the same bar. This time, an inebriated Robert tried to barricade me against the bar to prevent me from dancing. I was shocked, angry, and hurt. I couldn't understand what I'd done wrong. I stormed out. Robert followed me to the hotel, and we rowed. "You cannot tell me what I can or can't do. I don't care how much money you have." He continued to hurl abuse at me before storming off. I frantically searched online for available flights back to Bristol Airport. There was no available commercial flight home for days; I was stuck in Jersey. After Robert showed remorse in the morning, and given I was trapped there with no way home, I decided the only thing to do was to try to make the best of an uncomfortable situation.

A remorseful Robert and I talked over breakfast. He said he was sorry; he didn't know what got into him. I accepted his apology at face value. He took me shopping and bought me an expensive bottle of Dior perfume. I decided it was best not to ruin the rest of the weekend and I didn't want to make matters worse. Besides shopping and lounging around the bars, we took a private vineyard tour and enjoyed fresh mussels at a waterfront restaurant in Jersey's picturesque marina.

As we flew back, I thought about a good friend's relationship with her abusive husband. First, he'd physically and emotionally abuse her, and then he'd shower her with gifts to say he was sorry. Quietly, I wondered about Robert. As I look back, I missed the signals. But at that moment, I was vulnerable, and company was the most important thing in the world. Robert made me believe I was his "princess."

~

Flower deliveries became a weekly occurrence; the florist joked, "I was a lucky girl." Despite Robert's wealth, I wanted him to understand my independent streak. I took turns paying for meals. Robert seemed to enjoy me paying despite his wads of cash. I also bought all the food and frequently cooked dinner at his house. We both recognized I was not interested in his money; I was more interested in companionship. It was far from love. I just hated being alone.

Robert was also good to Matthew. As promised, Robert arranged for Matthew to be his co-pilot. At the age of 13, my son flew his first plane with me and an excited Emily in the back seats!

We flew to Newquay in Devon and had lunch at Jamie Oliver's notorious Fifteen. One of the patrons asked where we lived. It was cool saying we'd just flown down from Bristol for lunch.

Emily quite enjoyed flying in a small plane, but later confessed she didn't like Robert one bit. "There's something about him," she would say. I should have listened to my daughter. I'll never make the same mistake again.

~

September flew by. I supported Robert at the funeral of a close friend and tried to get on with my life. I relaunched my Etsy shop selling homemade soaps and bath bombs, had new hair extensions, joined the school mums for dinner, and took the kids for dinner with Robert. Soon, Emily's annual cheer award night came along. She was awarded the trophy for Most Improved Cheerleader. It was half the size of her, and she was beaming. It made me sad that her father did not attend.

One evening over a glass of wine, Robert asked me a question, "Do you have a specific bucket list destination?"

The answer was easy; "The Maldives. Ever since my parents had gone for an anniversary and I'd seen the pictures. John planned to take me for my 40th birthday."

"Guess that's not going to happen," he replied.

"Very astute," I smiled.

"When do you want to go?" he asked casually.

I wasn't sure if he was serious.

"Consider it done," he added.

I know he was trying to impress me, but what girl doesn't want to be spoilt? The trip made it official. I was Anastasia in *50 Shades of Grey*. I could raise a hand in the air and shout, "Hey world, I'm moving on and with a bloody millionaire!" Deep down, that was far from what I'd wanted but I felt as though I was stuck in sinking mud and there was no easy way out.

The Maldives trip was expensive; £10,000 for the bungalow on the lagoon, jet fares, and seaplane transfers. Then there were the expenses at the resort.

~

Robert's behavior changed as we got closer to departure. He was trying to treat me as his loyal subject. The tension built. He took to shouting. I'd handed back the keys to his house and left.

But he apologized profusely and lured me back. Robert had his claws in me and would not let me go. We were opposites; he craved control, and I didn't like to upset people about anything. I reluctantly agreed to go on holiday. "Just be careful," warned my friend Mary.

The night before we left, we had Matthew's birthday meal as a family. I joked to John that he was off the hook for my 40th birthday. I also told him that I didn't want to go to the Maldives with Robert. "Don't then," he said bluntly.

Deep in my heart, I'd again hoped he would say, "Don't. Please come back to me!" But John never ever fought for me; he wasn't about to start now. I had to accept that.

With a knot in my stomach, a tear in my eye, and filled with conflicting emotions, Robert and I headed for Heathrow airport.

I had no idea the surprises that awaited me in paradise.

34.

PARADISE LOST

"The mind is its own place, and itself can make a heaven of hell, a hell of heaven."

— John Milton

2018…

The Maldives was a lesson in truth. When something seems too good to be true, it is. Period! Full Stop!

Unknown to Robert, Mum and I had a face-to-face talk hours before we left. She did not mince her words. "Vicki," yelled Mum, "I hear that dirty old man has a violent temper!"

At that moment, I believed, Mum would say anything to stop me from going to the Maldives with a man more than ten years older than me. I didn't realize she was trying to protect her fragile daughter from potential harm.

"Who told you that?" I screeched.

"Lots of people! I've been told he can be a nasty, nasty man."

"Mum, I'm a 37-year-old woman. I'm perfectly capable of taking care of myself."

Her response cut deep, "You can't really believe that? It's laughable. You're vulnerable, and he's a disgusting pig!"

"At least he's taking good care of me, Mum, and I'm not alone." I replied, then stormed out of her house. I knew there was zero chance of changing Mum's mind. I was also so blinded by his attention that I never looked and saw what he was hiding behind his back.

Robert and I flew to Istanbul, then took a connecting flight to the Maldives. The first flight was filled with elegant little touches; the second had private booths with desks and comfy beds.

We arrived in the rain. Seaplanes could not take off for hours. When the skies cleared, I took a snapshot of us by the seaplane and eagerly climbed on board. We flew over the most beautiful islands nestled amid turquoise oceans. It was heaven on earth.

It was too choppy to land at the hotel. We moored in the sea, stepped onto a pontoon, and were collected by a boat. It felt surreal.

We looked happy; another couple asked if we were on our honeymoon. "No, we've just met," I laughed.

I could feel the stares: we were *Beauty and the Beast*. Why would a young woman spend her time with an older man like him? I didn't care what anyone thought, my heart was beating, and the cracks were healing. What better place to put me back together, than the Maldives?

~

If the Maldives was paradise, tiny Coco Island was like heaven in paradise. Robert had booked a sea and beach villa to enjoy the best of both worlds. But within an hour of arrival, he decided to spend another £5,000 to upgrade to a pool villa with a huge jacuzzi bathroom opening onto the deck with a private infinity pool overlooking azure waters, and a personal butler 24/7. It was like nothing I'd ever seen.

Robert was tired from the travel through time zones and opted to get some sleep. I'd went to the beach with a book and collected some shells for Emily. I watched couples, hand in hand, kissing in the ocean, and despite being in paradise, I felt alone. How could you come to such a magical place and sleep in bed for half the day? I couldn't understand his logic.

Our first night was magical: a great meal, followed by drinks and dancing on our private balcony to Chris De Burgh's *Lady in Red*. He seemed to genuinely care about pleasing me.

On day two, things quickly fell apart. After a fun evening, I'd posted pictures on Facebook of the island, our room, plus a few selfies. Friends demanded a few couple pics. As the requests continued, I decided to share a picture of us by the seaplane on Instagram. That's when, the shit hit the fan!

Robert's ex, who'd been demanding to know my identity, saw the picture. She emailed Robert and listed everything she could find out about my life—creepy!

~

Robert shouted; said he'd wanted to keep me a secret to protect me from her. "What the fuck!" he stomped "You should have asked my permission to post the picture of us."

I was stunned; I thought he would feel happy that I was proud to share a picture of us publicly. I agreed to remove it, I felt terrible for upsetting him and causing issues. But the WIFI was rubbish, so I went to the villa. Robert stayed at the bar drinking. I was upset, and felt I was being unfairly stalked by his crazy ex.

I deleted the picture, then opened the minibar and drank a glass of wine. In anger, I messaged the ex, asked her to "Kindly stop looking up my life and allow us to enjoy the holiday." She must have contacted Robert AGAIN. He returned to the room like a raging bull.

Robert tried dragging me off the pontoon steps. I broke free and walked into the sea in my bikini to get away. I stayed in the ocean for 15-20 minutes, too afraid to go back. But I couldn't stay there forever; the stingrays were swimming closer. Quietly, I returned to our bungalow and sat on the steps. Robert came out and picked me up, carrying me in his arms as I wept. I thought he was sorry. He didn't speak; he just pushed me face down on the bed and pinned me down. He yanked my bikini bottoms down and struck me repeatedly. I screamed, begged him to stop, told him he was hurting me. But he kept hitting and hitting me over and over and over. I lay there completely immobile. "You need to be taught a lesson," he screeched. I sobbed until it was over and lay frozen as he walked onto the balcony. Terrified, I curled into a ball. I feared that he would return for a second round, but he just sat and stared out at the ocean.

~

Robert ordered me to stop crying, as the neighbors would hear. He was like Dr. Jekyll and Mr. Hyde. After an hour or so, he apologized, claiming his physical assault was intended to be sexual. I didn't buy the twisted lie. He had administered a violent onslaught that I didn't deserve. Robert insisted we go for dinner; he was unbelievably scary.

"Come on get dressed and we'll go for dinner."

Stunned, I did not answer. He glared at me, then smiled. It was unreal behavior. I wondered if he had a split personality disorder.

There was nothing I could do. I was stranded in the Indian Ocean and would need a seaplane to escape. I agreed to join Roger for dinner to keep the peace. I imagined Mum saying, "I told you so."

The remainder of "the vacation" was strained. I spent days reading on the beach, wandering and enjoying the tranquillity while Robert slept, hoping that he would sleep even longer. When he was awake, Robert enjoyed putting his hands tight around my throat. I told him I didn't like it. He'd stop for a brief moment, and then his hands would wander back. He wanted complete control over me. I also discovered he was into kinky shit—there was a dog collar in his bedside cabinet. I tried to dismiss it since he'd had already told me his ex-girlfriend liked it rough.

What the hell was I thinking? Could I be that stupid?

35.

THE MODEL & THE THUG

"It is not the bruises on the body that hurt. It is the wounds of the heart and the scars on the mind."

— Aisha Mirza

2018…

Wake up! The grass is rarely greener somewhere else.

I was sunbathing in one of the most beautiful places in the world with a man who was spoiling me. It should have been a piece of heaven on this earth. Robert's disturbing behavior erased all that. The first days had been the trip to hell filled with bizarre and contradictory images that would be hard to erase. I should have been there with my soulmate, and Robert certainly wasn't that.

I hoped things would get better. They didn't. Robert fell ill. He had the chills and stomach cramps and became vile. Every waking minute was like walking on eggshells. Despite his oddities, I tried to be the better person and help nurse him back to health. Robert went to see the doctor, who prescribed some medications. Then I walked to the other side of the island to buy medication, but the shop was closed for lunch. I waited until they reopened. When I returned, he growled, why did I take so long? A few pills later, he was fast asleep. As I learned, the side effect of the meds was drowsiness. That meant Robert would sleep more than ever.

~

I decided I might as well make the most of our amenities. I used my phone timer to take snaps while I stood by the infinity pool above the ocean. I posted the pictures to my Facebook friends because I knew I'd probably never visit the Maldives again, and I wanted to show the world I was enjoying my new life. It was a lie of course!

Eventually, Robert showed signs of recovery. He suggested spa treatments followed by a private boat tour. "I brought you here for a good time; I want to make good on that promise," he said.

The vacation turned idyllic. We island hopped to a local village and school, where I bought a shell handbag for Emily, and a handmade bracelet with pearls for myself. We ate some fabulous local fish and drank cocktails. Robert even found a swing at the tip of the sea; it was picture perfect.

He also gave me permission for me to post a picture of us, which he captioned: "The model & the thug." Little did I know. Of all those happy times, I was in for twice as much hell.

~

Latino night arrived. I'd missed the beach party when he was ill, so I wanted the last night to be memorable. It was.

I told Robert I wanted to Facetime my children. He smiled, "Go for it." Unfortunately, the Wi-Fi connection was dreadful; I spent over 20 minutes trying to complete a single chat. I returned to Robert at the bar. The phone rang almost immediately. "Christ answer the damn thing!" he demanded.

"I can't hear them, the connection's terrible here.," I replied. "I'll go to the lobby to call them back." As I spoke, the phone continued to ring.

"Answer it now!" he replied angrily.

I said, "Sorry?"

"You heard me, answer the fucking phone!"

Robert had been drinking to excess. I told him to stop ordering me about; the fire in his eyes suggested my request was not well received. I got up, went to the lobby, called home and spoke to the children. They were happy I was having a good time, and I was happy they were well. I returned to our table to sit and enjoy the music.

"We're going. Come on!" Robert ordered. He had drunk my cocktail.

"Why did you drink my cocktail?" I asked.

He just laughed and stuck his hand out. "Come on; we're going."

"No, it's not even 9 pm. I'm going to stay, listen to music, and have a drink."

Robert stormed off. He wasn't used to people standing up to his bully boy behavior. I thought he realized from our last spat; I didn't respond well to being told what to do. A few drinks later, I returned to the room. Music was blasting and Robert was in the pool. He asked me to get in with him. I shook my head, no, and went to bed.

~

When I awoke, Robert was fast asleep. I went outside on the decking. My friend Mary had texted. I explained how the night had unfolded. She sensed I felt unsafe.

"If anything happens to me, know that it was him, not me," I warned. I slipped back into bed. Mary texted back. The phone made a noise, and the screen illuminated.

"What the hell are you doing?" screeched Robert, now awakened.

"I'm replying to a message."

"Stop fucking making noise."

He was unbelievable. I got out of bed to retrieve water from the fridge.

"What the fuck are you doing now?"

"I'm just getting some water," I replied calmly.

"I told you, bitch, stop making fucking noise."

I couldn't help myself at that point. "When I get home, I'm going to tell people what you're really like." That was it. I'd crossed the line.

Robert jumped out of bed, waving his arms and pointing his finger in my face like a thug. "You're nothing but a fucking whore, you deserve to have your hair ripped out of your fucking head," he screamed. His eyes were wild, almost insane. I'd never felt so afraid. He started pushing and shoving me backward.

"Stop it, please. Why are you being like this? Can I please get into the safe for my wallet and passport?"

"I'm going to rip up your fucking passport. Try getting home, bitch!" He shoved me into the bathroom sink. I winced in pain. He continued coming at me as a man possessed.

"Stop it, please!" I begged, putting my hands in front of my face.

Robert ignored my pleas, charged with balled fists, grabbed hold of my wrist, and threw me into the doorframe. My bracelet snapped, and the pearls scattered. I stumbled across the table and landed on the decking like a ragdoll. He stood over me as I lay curled into a ball on the deck. "You're a fucking pathetic bitch, you hear me? Remember, I didn't touch you. Understand?" After assaulting and humiliating me, he walked away and went back to bed, like nothing ever happened, leaving me frightened to death on the floor.

I realized if he assaulted me again, he had the brute strength to kill me. I wouldn't stand a chance, so I lay motionless until I was certain he'd fallen back to sleep. It took guts, but I peeled myself off the floor, grabbed my phone, and crept back inside. I texted Mary again, telling her what happened.

"FFS. Leave now," she ordered. "Go, find help. You can go back with security in the morning for your belongings."

Mary was right, but I was petrified at the thought of being caught fleeing and enduring another vicious beating. My twisted pride entered. If I was going to die, I needed John to know that I was not responsible, Robert was.

I texted John: "I've made a huge mistake. My life is in danger; if I don't make it home, please let the kids know I love them so very much."

There was no reply from John. What the hell did I expect?

36.

ABUSED AND INTIMIDATED

"No matter how much we try, no matter how much we want it ... some stories just don't have a happy ending."
— Jodi Picoult

2018…

The memories of being physically abused last a lifetime, maybe longer.

I wandered around the hotel looking for help, but everyone was asleep. I sat on a sunbed in the darkness with a throbbing arm under the stars until daybreak. Robert's violent ways had taken the skin off my arm and elbow. My arm was swollen; it felt broken.

At 6.30 am, I snuck back inside the room to grab my wallet from the safe to pay for the doctor's visit. Robert had changed the combination. I lay on the decking in agony. Robert woke at about 8 am. I waited for another 15 minutes, took a deep breath, then ventured inside to ask him for the safe combination. He slammed the terrace door in my face as he railed, "How many times do I fucking need to tell it to you, no?"

"Sorry, but I need my wallet to see the doctor. I think you've broken my arm."

Robert laughed and raised his eyebrows. "I didn't fucking touch you. It's all in your head."

I argued. "The cuts and bruises say otherwise."

He knew exactly how to bring my worst fears to the forefront. He was vile and crazy. "Tell anyone, anything, and I'll have you committed. I'll tell everyone you just make up shit! Who do you think they'll believe? Don't forget; I know about your unstable history. I'll make sure the authorities take your kids from you." I was stunned.

He finally let me into the safe. I grabbed my wallet and visited the medic, who examined the bruises on my arms and legs, and placed my arm in a sling. The medic believed there was a chance my arm was broken, but I'd need an x-ray at the mainland hospital to confirm his diagnosis. His recommendation required seaplane transport, hours of waiting, and a complicated itinerary reroute. "If it turns out to be broken, the airline may not allow you to fly," he warned.

The medic suggested I waited to get proper medical treatment from a hospital in the UK. I agreed. He prescribed strong pain killers and a pain gel to rub on my arm during the return trip.

When I returned to the room in the sling, Robert rolled his eyes. I went out onto the terrace, stared out to sea, and cried. Robert knew he was in the wrong and was playing songs with apologies in the lyrics. Then he put on swimming shorts, walked outside, and said, "Let's draw a line under last night, okay?" He wanted me to wipe the night from my memory—he was crazy!

"Get in the pool and immerse your arm," he ordered. I refused. He reminded me he still had my passport. I got in; he swam over to me. I wanted to vomit; I couldn't bear being close to him. Minutes later, we got out, and he sat beside me, trying to rub the pain gel on my arm. It made my skin crawl.

~

Our butler moved us to a courtesy room for the afternoon and took our belongings. I sat on the deck sobbing before going for a lie down on the bed. Suddenly Robert appeared and tried to fondle me.

I pushed him off. "Do you think I'd be intimate with you after what you did to me?" I made it crystal clear. He was never going to lay a finger on me ever again. Mr. Hyde got the message; Dr. Jekyll reappeared, "How about we go for some lunch? No need to travel on an empty stomach."

I painted on my best smile, "Sounds good." I rationalized I'd soon be home, and never have to see Dr. Jekyll or Mr. Hyde again.

After lunch, the shit hit the fan, again. I'd posted a picture, for evidence purposes, of me in a sling, saying: "Not how I planned to spend my last day." I hadn't said Robert had done it; I just wanted a record to show I'd been injured in the Maldives. Someone—probably his ex—told him. He flew off the handle again, shouted in my face.

We boarded the seaplane in silence and arrived at the airport hours before the connecting flight check-in. After all the shouting and threats, he remained oddly silent for three hours. I was in severe pain; the tablets were making me sweat, and I felt dizzy. He bought some water. Then the crazy bastard put my head onto his shoulder and started singing. I bit my tongue and allowed him to stroke my hair. At check-in, he gave our passports to the staff for processing, then he disappeared and left me in the business lounge. I frantically messaged friends begging someone, anyone, to meet me at the airport so I could flee Robert's satanical grip.

~

Once on board, I quickly turned my seat into a bed. I figured if I closed my eyes and pretended to sleep, I wouldn't have to look at or speak to him. My skin was filled with goosebumps as he tucked me in with blankets and stroked my hair. He believed I'd forgiven him. I hadn't. I wouldn't. How stupid did he think I was?

At Istanbul, while waited for our final journey leg in the lounge; Robert's cell phone rang. I knew it was his ex. Robert walked away, took the call. He returned, furious, and began to spew obscenities.

"You fucking bitch! Why did you post that picture?"

"You're lucky I didn't tell people that you did it to me," I responded. "Perhaps I should tell your father what sort of a man his son is?" That got me into more trouble. Robert threw my passport at me and said, "You're on your own from here, bitch."

Thankfully, the ticket was inside. I boarded the plane and felt sick knowing we would be sitting next to each other. Robert glared, "I suggest you find another seat; I don't want to hear any more shit that comes out of your mouth."

I would not give him the satisfaction of moving seats and instead turned away and stared out of the window all the way back to Heathrow. I could not wait to be free of him. When we landed, my phone wouldn't work. I was petrified. In a moment of kindness, Robert told me how to reboot it. Then he said, "If you're coming with me, I suggest you keep your mouth shut, act jovial, and don't bring my staff into our shit."

There was no way I'd get into a car with him. "No thanks." I grabbed my case, and I walked away. My heart was hammering in my chest a thousand beats per minute. I'd had the guts to stand up to him.

I saw him lurking in the arrivals area, waiting for me. All the trains had been canceled, and a bus would take 11 hours. My sister Shelly rang as I sobbed, trying to figure out what to do. Shelly told me she had called John.

"You didn't."

"I did. He was sympathetic," said Shelly. "You'll see."

The phone rang, it was John. "I'm so sorry. I didn't realize how bad things were."

I replied, "Didn't you get my text that my life was in danger?"

I could feel the frustration on the other end. "Vicki, I didn't realise that you were in danger."

John had booked a £250 UBER taxi to bring me home to the kids. I knew it was an act of kindness, not love. My knight in shining armour would never love me again, particularly after all this.

As the Uber left the airport, Robert texted, "Are you coming?" I smiled, feeling proud of myself for walking away, and replied. "I'm long gone."

37.
THE BOBBY VAN

"Courage doesn't mean you don't get afraid.
Courage means you don't let fear stop you."
— Bethany Hamilton

2018...

There is a fine line for the woman who stands up to a bully. She can be labeled a role model or held in contempt by the opposite sex.

I survived! I was on home ground, albeit battered and bruised. I cannot express the relief that I felt in that Uber. The ride home seemed to last forever, but I was home. Mum and Shelly embraced me, relieved that I'd escaped Robert's violent clutches. Relaying the details of my trip was traumatising and embarrassing. Mum was kind, she never once said, "I told you so."

Collecting Emily at school with my arm in a sling was equally embarrassing. I waited for her in the playground before explaining what Robert had done to Mummy.

For weeks after, I was a shell of my former self. I was living with the fear, that one day, Robert would come knocking. I wondered how many women/ex-wives he had abused. I doubted I was the first and believed I wouldn't be the last to experience his violent temper.

My neighbor, a school mum, was a shoulder to cry on, someone I trusted and admired. She convinced me that Robert should be held accountable. "He shouldn't be allowed to get away with it," she advised. It was a tough decision to do the right thing; he was rich and powerful; I was just me. It was like David versus Goliath.

I decided to report the assaults online. The next day, two police officers visited my house and asked me to talk them through my ordeal. It was traumatic, and again, embarrassing, telling them how he'd pinned me down and repeatedly struck my backside, and threw me through a door.

To my surprise, they were good listeners and informed me that Robert had a thick police file. I wanted to vomit. No details could be released, but they insinuated he had several previous violations for violence. I cried tears of joy. Charges would be brought; two counts of common assault or actual bodily harm, plus intimidation. An arrest would be made after my official statement, and he'd be brought in for questioning.

I was pleased and satisfied that justice might be done. I was also petrified. Once the charges were brought, I feared Robert would try to retaliate, and I'd end up hurt or beaten to death.

The officers understood my predicament. They alerted The Bobby Van scheme (Police locksmiths who secure vulnerable people's homes) to secure my house with window and door alarms and a sturdy door chain. I was also given a personal attack alarm.

The Bobby Van man came that same day—normally, such matters could take up to ten days. I was told the officers placed a rush on perimeter protection since they felt there might be an immediate threat, given Robert's prior behavior.

I wondered why all this had happened to me. Was it punishment for a lifetime of failed choices? I was blamed publicly, by a so-called friend, on my Facebook page for agreeing to go away with him so soon. No one deserves a beating for stupidity! My children heard my story first-hand. They were furious. Matthew wanted to egg his house with his mates, bless him. I discouraged him. "Robert will get more than an egging once the cops are done with him."

~

The phone rang at 8 am the following morning. "I'm sorry, Mrs. FitzGerald, my sergeant says we can't bring charges due to lack of jurisdiction in the Maldives." He was telling me Avon & Somerset Police had no legal authority to press charges. It was up to the Maldives Police. Mr Grey would get away with his crimes! I was deflated and pissed off. I took to social media to post pictures of all my injuries. Robert was not named, but everyone demanded I expose his identity, publicly, and shame the public figure for who he really was.

I was certain Robert would sue me. He spent half his life defending legal claims. He had both the means and experience. I was right. Threats arrived in my email. He sent a Non-Molestation order to prevent me from ever exposing him. I was intimidated by the legalese. I'd done nothing wrong; the police officer said I was within my rights to post such pictures. As an intimidation tactic, Robert broke with accepted procedure and sent the court papers to me directly, instead of filing them with the court. The bastard was relentless.

~

Days passed. Every time I was home alone, I feared he would turn up. A few texts came; a picture of a new elaborate mansion and messages saying I'd always be his princess. It was crazy. I could see why women get drawn back, especially when you're vulnerable and lonely. I never thought I would become a victim of domestic abuse. It ruined me. My confidence was shattered.

Getting away with the kids was my only escape. I wanted to heal with the two people I loved most in this world. We flew to Faro, Portugal, where I took the kids for tapas, shopped in boutiques, and played at the waterpark. I pretended that I was fine and recovered.

Robert was never punished for what he did to me, but Karma did step in. Six months after the incident, he lost his seat in the council elections. To add insult to injury, after the election, the council leader offered a proposal to have Robert completely removed from his political party, but to this day, he has not been successful. I have no doubt that, in time, Robert will see jail time if he abuses another woman. You can't get away with your crimes forever.

I may have been unsuccessful in getting justice due to jurisdiction, but I've got a message for every woman, and man, for that matter who feels they have been abused or intimidated by a partner, *Go get 'em! Don't let the vicious brutes get away with it. The best person to stand up for you is you!*

38.

Bumbling for Mr. Right

"Love is like a fairy tale. Some people find happiness in the first person they meet. Others have to kiss a lot of frogs."
— Anonymous

2018…

Sometimes identifying Mr. Right requires a little creativity.

With all the craziness surrounding the men in my life, I was understandably apprehensive about seeking new male companionship. I hibernated instead.

"Get yourself on Bumble!" insisted my friend, Gina.

"What the hell is Bumble?" I asked.

"Online dating, but the girls are in charge!"

"No bloody way!" I responded indignantly. I had sworn during my worst days that if I were ever single, I would never go swiping. I'd seen enough *dick pics* when Lara was eating men alive with her sex addiction.

Gina persisted. "You need a distraction. It's fun: it will make you forget John and take your mind off all the bad shit that's happened to you. It's how I met my Rick!"

Rick was the current love of Gina's life. He was a rugged DJ and chef with a wild side that had attracted my outspoken, laugh-a-minute girlfriend. Her enthusiasm was infectious. As I sat and wondered, my two alter egos did battle within my mind.

On my left shoulder sat conservative Vicki. She whispered, "Take a pass. Bumble is full of murderers, rapists, and other assorted weirdos." On my other shoulder sat naïve Nelly. She said, "You're not going to find Mr. Right if you don't look for Mr. Right." Nelly won the battle of the minds.

I went online to view Bumble with a bottle of rosè nearby. Two glasses of wine later, I signed up. The idea of the Bumble app—you had to like someone, if they liked you, then you got a BOOM match. Girls had 24 hours to make contact.

Random guys couldn't just message me, so I thought, why not, I'm sad and alone, what's there to lose? There were some oddballs, but equally, there were some hunks. It would be like looking for the needle in a haystack. And like Gina said, good distractions had the potential to lessen my fear of being alone.

I followed the directions and signed up, putting my best foot forward. Matches came fast and furious. I grew some balls and made the first move. It took concentration, so I didn't muddle them up. Online daters talk to multiple people, but I was new to this! I had never dated online; it didn't exist when I was single. Times change, it had been 20 years after all. In my day, you met a man at the pub or clubbing.

~

"The trick is to keep your options open; don't settle too quick," counseled Gina.

As I discovered, some guys said hi, then asked for bikini or topless pictures! I quickly deleted those dirtballs. In time, I identified three nice guys. They all wanted to meet in person, on the same day! It was naughty but fun. I had a drink at lunchtime with one, ice skated with another, and had evening drinks with the third. That would allow me to save time by comparing all three while they were fresh in my mind.

Date One - pub. A loud, confident Scot. His pictures were dated. Nice man but he pounced on me in the car park. Conclusion - Frog.

Date Two - ice skating. It was raining hard by the time I arrived; my curls were limp, and I looked like a drowned rat! Hugh looked as hot as his picture with a nice smile and pearly teeth. We skated and chatted. It seemed like I'd known him for years. He wanted to know my story. I was open and honest. He didn't run. Then he dropped a bomb; he was going to Germany for three months! So that was that! No frog, just bad timing.

Date Three - pub. Ric, as handsome as his pictures. Charming, funny, great smile, and smartly dressed. He ticked all the boxes. We had a lot in common; two children for one, which I liked, as it meant we both had baggage.

"Wish I'd kissed you goodbye," Ric texted on my way home. "I think we should stop driving and kiss." I laughed but wanted to kiss him too. We pulled into the Harvester pub and kissed in the car park. It wasn't classy! But it was fun! We had two further consecutive dinner dates and then he announced he was off to Dubai for business.

I was gutted; the situation was starting to sound like John all over again. But while overseas, Ric frequently messaged and Skyped. We both felt the chemistry. I felt myself getting swept away. Was Ric my new prince charming?

Time flew. Ric enjoyed me sending silly Snapchats. It became our thing; it made him laugh. He had succeeded in making me forget my baggage. I drove three hours to Heathrow to pick him up. He bought me flowers. It all seemed too good to be true. It was.

I wasn't supposed to be happy! I was the Black Widow, after all! One evening while Ric was away, I helped a builder friend of mine, Max, select wood slabs for my home project. It was a Friday and the kids were spending the weekend with their father. So, Max and I ended up at a pub. Despite being tipsy, Max insisted on driving us home.

Once Ric heard about the pub stop and car ride with Max, our dynamics changed dramatically. He wondered if I'd been unfaithful. I told him I had not. He was jealous, and I was confused; things had been going so well. Soon, I discovered Ric had a close relative who was seriously injured by a drunk driver. I also learned Ric carried other baggage: he was still in love with his ex-girlfriend, who had dumped him.

I decided it was time to move on.

~

Hugh (Date Two) messaged me out of the blue. He'd finished a course and wanted me to pop in for a cup of tea. I told him I was sweaty from a workout at the gym. He said it didn't matter. He was not in his Sunday best; he'd been working on a home improvement project on his balcony. He was persistent; I said, "What the hell." I drank tea while he finished working on his balcony. Even in overalls, he looked hot.

From there, our friendship grew. We met up for walks along the seafront; he was great at talking, almost like a therapist. He even cooked for me. We also became movie night buddies. One night after watching *Jigsaw*, we decided to go back to the beginning and watch all six Saw horror films. Soon that became our thing - Saw and rhubarb gin nights. I enjoyed spending time with him. There was a physical attraction, but I thought of it as more of friendship until the night he unexpectedly leaned over and kissed me. His lips were warm, inviting, and tender. I was confused. Had we crossed the line? I still wasn't sure.

~

Hugh was about to turn 40. I took him out for cocktails and dinner and bought him a make-your-own gin cake. During dinner, he casually announced he was off to Milan with his ex-girlfriend for a few days as 'friends.' Hugh said *she* invited herself. I wondered what the hell was it with these exes? Was I destined to be a permanent Number Two?

When he returned, we hung out like nothing ever happened. He bought me rhubarb gin, and I bought him a warm scarf for Christmas. Slowly, it became clear we were just not meant to be. Hugh wanted a new adventure in Germany with no long-distance ties. In the blink of an eye, Hugh was history. We spoke a couple times. It became clear that a new life overseas was what Hugh needed.

A question lingered in the back of my mind. Would I ever be able to meet enough frogs to discover my new prince charming?

I didn't realize that I already had.

39.

MILK TRAY MAN

"Love comes unexpectedly and feels like magic though your heart."

— Mhar Jurry

2018...

No one wants to be alone or single during the Christmas holiday; it sucks.

I had no prince on the horizon. Or so I thought. It turned out I'd already met an admirer; I just didn't realize it. Sometimes I'm surprisingly naïve.

As I sat watching the telly, my mind flashed back to the pub where Max and I drank after choosing wood for a wine cellar project. I noticed a tall, dark, handsome stranger at the bar. He was 6 ft 4 inches. I was worried the poor guy would hit his head on the low beams. He walked over, joined us, and introduced himself.

"Alright? I'm Simon."

"This is Vicki," Max answered.

Simon spoke with a deep preppy voice, stared at me with intoxicating eyes, and offered a gorgeous smile. He looked like the tough James Bond-style television figure, Milk Tray Man, who took on daunting 'raids' to surreptitiously deliver a box of chocolates to a lady. The TV hero made women all over England squeal and swoon.

Mark informed Simon that we'd been out to choose wood for my home project. The project never came to fruition though as Mark ended up in jail—but that's another story!

Simon explained he had only moved to Wrington that day, and it was his first night out in the area. I remember thinking, fate collided us. We began to chat. Simon mentioned he was going on a date the next day in Maidenhead. I was secretly gutted!

I suggested, "You should take some flowers, girls love flowers."

Apparently, as I gave my point of view, I accidentally placed my hand on Simon's knee. "Friend me on Facebook," he said, casually. I only knew his first name, which yielded ridiculous results, and he wasn't on Max's friends' list. I gave up. After all, he had already told me he was dating!

~

Two weeks later Max became friends with Simon on Facebook. Soon, I received a friend request from Simon too, who said he'd been hoping I'd find him. He thought my accidental touch was a signal, and it never occurred to him that I assumed he was already dating.

Shortly after, Max confessed in a text to me that he'd tried to harm himself due to issues in his personal life. His son had found him with a noose around his neck attempting to hang himself.

Having been through tough dark times, I wanted to help. I told Max to come meet me and the children and join us for dinner at my local. We then drove to a country pub called The White Hart, in the nearby village of Wrington. I didn't want him to be alone. Loneliness messes with the mind and disturbs your thoughts. I'd been there too many times.

Max was a broken man. His ex was taking him to court after they got into a fight, and he wasn't coping with life. As we entered the pub, I noticed my handsome stranger, Simon, was at the bar. I felt a little giddy. When he looked at me and spoke, it gave me butterflies, as though my heart had been revived by a defibrillator charge. There was something mysterious and sexy about him. Such a god damn shame he was already dating!

~

Simon and I chatted outside while he had a smoke. I was freezing and shivering under my black woolen coat but put a brave face on. As we talked, I told him in confidence what Max had tried to do with regards to ending his life and asked him to kindly keep an eye on him.

During the conversation, Simon told me that he'd wanted to take me out, but Max had given him a firm "no." I was shocked. Why had Max decided to butt into my personal affairs. It was none of his damn business!

I laughed nervously, a little taken aback by the disclosure; I reiterated that Max and I were just friends. Max interrupted us; the conversation became awkward. Max insisted on driving me home. Simon messaged to ask if everything was okay. I responded, "yes," assuming he was trying to be friendly. A few messages followed, then he reeled me in with a hook. "I know you're an author. I've got an idea for a book; it's based on a true story about a millionaire trying to kill his girlfriend with a sawed-off shotgun!" Intrigued, I agreed to meet. He told me he would bring the newspaper clippings and I should bring a pad and pen!

~

When Simon picked me up, I was uncertain as to his intentions; was this a business meeting or a date? Unsure, I decided to show my glam side. I curled my hair and wore an elegant teal off the shoulder long sleeve lace top, black jeans, and heels.

He also had made an effort to look sharp; in a posh coat, smart wool polo neck jumper, and jeans. I smiled to myself.

The story, revealed in Simon's newspaper clippings, was intriguing. A millionaire gaming machine dealer attempted to murder his young ex-girlfriend by driving up the cliff in his Porsche 911 Carrera armed with his shotgun. The woman jumped out of the car when he was forced to slow around a sharp turn. The man sped off with the shotgun still behind his seat. He either lost control on the wet road surface or deliberately crashed. The vehicle plunged about 1,000 feet down a cliff and landed on a rock plateau. Miraculously, the driver survived, and the shotgun was recovered by police, shortly before it burst into flames.

At this moment, I still believed we were just having an enjoyable business meeting about his gruesome story, despite the obvious chemistry. Two days later, he took me out for a roast dinner, which was equally enjoyable. On Christmas Day he wished me a Merry Christmas before I headed to Mum and Dad's.

On Boxing Day (the day after Christmas) my family was sitting around reminiscing when Simon messaged, asking my plans. I suggested we meet for a drink; I didn't like to think of him alone during the holidays. I met him at The Plough Inn, again in Wrington, in my little black dress. I was a mite overdressed for a county pub, but it was Christmas!

I didn't want to leave so soon, but I had to get back to the family. When I arrived, Mum was cross that I was 20 minutes late and had missed tea. I explained I had met a friend for a holiday drink, so he would not feel alone during Christmas. She nodded disapprovingly. What I didn't say to Mum was that I hoped that I'd see him again soon.

~

Dad took me aside to deliver his Christmas present to his princess. He said, "I don't think John wanted your marriage to end." He explained that was the reason he seemingly ignored my suggestion about the next logical step after separation—filing for divorce. Dad continued, "Everyone in the family wants the two of you to get back together." I was shocked and confused. I could not see John and me together again. I didn't want to put myself through the torment of living that old lonely life again despite a part of me still loving him. As a responsible mum, I thought I should go back for the sake of the children and make the kids and my family happy. Isn't that what proper parents do, stay together for the kids?

I needed closure. Feeling brave, I had *the* divorce conversation with John over the phone. Dad was dead wrong; neither John nor I could see a bright future together.

Interestingly, he left it to me to take the lead in filing for divorce. I told him I wanted to move on with my life and stop dwelling on the past. Teary-eyed, I looked around as I walked along Weston seafront by myself. I was surrounded by happy families and kids with their new bikes and scooters.

I was frightened and alone with an uncertain future ahead.

40

MUM, PLEASE COME HOME

"Suicide doesn't take the pain away. It just passes it on to others and breaks hearts."

— Matthew FitzGerald

2018…

I made a New Year's resolution. Vicki would toss her fragility to the wind and start life anew.

I drove to North Wales and collected a puppy! It was crazy, but it seemed like the kids and I needed a new addition. I was supposed to meet Simon later that evening for dinner but couldn't leave a new puppy alone.

We arranged to go to my favourite Greek restaurant, Dimitris, the following night. Initially, I felt apprehensive about being seen in Dimitris with a man that wasn't my husband. Dimitri would be stunned for sure—he'd only ever known me as married to John. But there I was, dressed to kill in a sexy black lace and navy bodycon dress.

Once again, I was overthinking matters. Nobody cared. We enjoyed another fabulous night. I found Simon charming, and he made me smile, something that I needed. He asked my plans for New Year's Eve. I told him, "I've been invited to a friend's house party." He was openly disappointed.

~

A day later, December 30, Mum invited me and the children for lunch. Matthew would not get off the Xbox. Out of frustration, I issued several warnings. "You better get off that thing, we are going to be late. If you don't come now, you'll have to cycle there." He ignored me, thinking I'd never follow up on my threat. Dinner was at 1pm; it was 12.55pm. Matthew arrived at Mum's on his bike like a wild devil. Mum was horrified at his language.

"It's no wonder Dad doesn't want you!" he bellowed.

I'd never heard him speak in that way, and I was upset. I shouted,

"You rude little boy, how dare you speak to your mother like that!" Then I confiscated his phone and banned his Xbox.

Dinner was awkward, to say the least. Mum had her own gripes; "You and your sister never take me anywhere." Frustrated at her insensitivity, I probably said something I should not have.

"Don't you realize, right now, I'm just trying to get from one day to the next?" There was an awkward silence at the table. I felt that I was not good enough as a daughter.

~

Upset, and feeling like no one loved me, I made another dark decision; I'd drive to Sand Bay and walk into the mudflats.

The further I got, the greater the cracks became in the mudflats. I had to run and jump to the next. Then I noticed the tide was going out—I couldn't get anything right. I turned back to shore and laid on the rocks, thinking. My phone rang; it was Matthew. I refused to tell him where I was and said some terrible things. "You know you made Mummy leave. You're old enough to know, actions have consequences. You need to think before you hurt somebody with your words."

After a long silence, Matthew began to cry and apologize over the phone, "Mum, I'm really sorry. Please come home." I knew he meant it. I hung up, embarrassed. It was unfair of me to say what I said to my 13-year-old son. I'll never forgive myself for that.

~

First, Simon messaged. "I'm concerned about you, give me a ring, let's talk it out over a drink." I felt I didn't know him well enough then to confide. He must have thought I was having a meltdown, but he still wanted to come to my aid.

Suddenly a text appeared from my old Bumble friend Ric. I replied saying that I was in a dark place. He became worried and said he was in his car coming to find me. "Turn on your damn What's App tracker, so I can find you." He also mentioned he had notified the local police. That was all I needed! If they found me, they would certainly detain me and have me labeled crazy and a danger to myself.

~

My sister Shelly joined in the recovery effort. She kept ringing, leaving voicemails, begging me to tell her where I was. What a mess I had created. I turned on the WhatsApp tracker on my mobile phone and staggered back to the road. Soon, I walked into my brother-in-law, Vince, sister Shelly, and Ric. People did care. They'd come to find me and tell me I needed to come home. Ric hugged me until I stopped shaking. "You silly girl." I'll never forget Ric for that night. He'd driven over 30 miles to find me, told the police all was well, then took me to my house where all of us sat around the kitchen table drinking a cup of tea. No one knew what to say.

A wise man once said, *"if you don't know what to say to someone who treats you kindly, just say thank you."*

41.
SECOND TIME AROUND

"Love is a lovelier the second time around. Makes you think perhaps that love, like youth, is wasted on the young."
— Frank Sinatra

2019…

It was time to let go; turn the page. Easier said than done when you're bruised and battered, emotionally and physically.

One thing was certain, I was far from feeling okay, but I was falling for the new gentleman in my life; Simon. The tall, dark, handsome, stranger, who, despite everything, wanted to spend time with me. I wondered was Karma done, was it time to experience happiness.

Simon made me feel good, something that had been missing for a very long time. He was wonderful, so sweet and so kind. He helped me to forget all the bad and put a smile back on my face. It was the way he looked at me, the way he spoke. Both sent tingles over my body. I never thought I'd find love again, but I was falling hard. He was funny, handsome, kind, and patient.

New Year's Eve was an example of his patience. I'd accepted two invitations, a quiet romantic Japanese dinner with Simon and a party at a friend's house. Dinner was magical, I didn't want it to end. So, when Simon stopped his fancy Mercedes G-Class outside her house, I was conflicted. I wanted him to accompany me, but my conservative English upbringing felt it was too soon. I wasn't ready to share Simon with my friends or for their comparisons to John. Even John's friend, Tom, advised me to keep a low profile, "I think it's best for all parties concerned—at least until things return to normal."

~

As the evening progressed, love filled Anna's house as everyone kissed and welcomed in the New Year. I stood alone at the edge of the dance floor. My thoughts turned to Simon; God! I had made a terrible mistake. Simon should have been at my side welcoming in the New Year. I also had another epiphany: things would never return to normal. Might Simon be my guide to a new normal?

I was filled with self-doubt. I'd lived in the darkest corner of a castle surrounded by an imaginary moat to protect myself from the disappointment of the world outside. Did I have the capacity to let another human being touch my heart? If I made another mistake or he tired of me, could I withstand the rejection?

I had no answers for my questions. All I knew was that Simon had knocked me for six (threw me off balance) when he entered my life. I was exhausted, searching for the old Vicki while playing Mum to my wonderful children. I ached all over, I wanted—no, I craved to be—loved, truly loved, imperfections and all.

~

Simon was different than any man I had ever met. He was extremely shy and that made him mysterious. I liked the fact that he wasn't arrogant or vain. He wasn't the confident corporate type; he was a hard-working man and had a demanding physical job as a scrap metal dealer. I wondered whether the saying was true; opposites attract. He loved cars and scrap; I was creative dreamer yearning for romance—we couldn't have been more different. Still, we did have some things in common; a love of laughter, great food and wine, a love of travel, nice clothes, and our dogs.

We wined, dined, and enjoyed ten romantic dates before he even kissed me on the cheek. I wondered, if I'd found myself a true gentleman. I was honest about my roller-coaster life to date and learned that he, too, had experienced the sadness of broken relationships and family bonds. Simon had endured a 15-year relationship and had since been living alone. I believed fate aligned us. We were both lost souls searching for happiness.

Taking it slow, made me want him even more. It was all in his game plan, of course. The first time we met, I'd said I was fed up with men pouncing, just because I was single. Simon wasn't stupid. He listened, made a mental note of that comment, and took time to woo me.

Simon got my heart pumping again; he warmed blood flowing in my icy veins and restored *that charming Vicki smile* that had been absent for so long. Fate had created a good match.

As we drove home one evening, Natasha Bedingfield's song, *Unwritten*, played on the radio. *"Live your life with arms wide open. Today is where your book begins, the rest is still unwritten."*

Her lyrics resonated—my life was beginning; the pen was in my hand. I would take the plunge on love, no matter the consequences. I'd write the next chapter of my life and live it with arms wide open. I secretly prayed the second time around would be better than the first.

Simon was becoming my bright morning sun rising over the hill. I was falling hard and wanted him to unlock the padlock around my heart. He was caring and sincere; he took the time to listen, to feel my pain and my heartache. The broken me tried to keep him at bay; she wasn't ready to be crushed again. But Simon persevered. He took this fragile little bird under his wing and nurtured her back to health with massive doses of love and kindness.

~

The first time we crossed the intimacy line, it was electric. He had raw passion. It was the way he looked at me, the way he kissed, touched, and made love to me. I felt alive. And when he held me in his arms, I felt safe.

Despite flying to Dublin for a girl's trip, I couldn't get Simon out of my head! When he called at the airport, saying he couldn't wait to see me, I realized I was under his spell. I thought to myself, maybe youth was, indeed, wasted on the young! I hoped God had decided I'd been punished enough. The moment we reunited, I felt like Julia Roberts in the movie *Notting Hill.* "I'm just a girl asking a boy to love her."

~

While we both longed to be happy again, we were afraid to take a leap through fear of being hurt. Sharing our feelings with one another, therefore, was a huge step—he's a man of few words. I can still remember the conversation when we went from dating to lovers. We were flirting over the phone. He was at home; I was with Anna.

"So, are we a couple now?"

I replied, "I don't know, are we?"

"I think we should be," he said.

"Does that mean we are?"

"Well, I'd like to be."

I beamed, "Well then, I guess we are."

Anna mocked us, "God you sound like a pair of school kids."

In a way, I felt as though I were an innocent teen starting out for the first time and experimenting with love. Truth was, I craved affection, having not felt loved for so many years. Simon made me happy, something I never thought I'd feel again after all the trauma. I found what I was looking for, and it felt good.

~

Simon cares but finds it difficult to share his emotions. I love it when he holds my hand, puts his arm around me, and pulls me close. (I wish he'd do it more). I also love that he enjoys making me breakfast in bed, cooking me dinners, and snuggling on the sofa, (even when it's Scrap Kings or car shows). I take an interest because everyone is different, and we all have our passions.

Simon is what us girls label, 'a bloke bloke'. He is not all hearts and flowers, he's set in his ways, doesn't like to break routine, and does lack the romantic streak you see in the movies, but I'm working on that. I'm hoping one day he'll give me flowers, dance with me, leave our footprints in the sand. I'm also working on myself.

Simon deserves a medal. I mean that. I've plenty of flaws, I'm far from perfect, have many emotional scars, but he still wants me even though I constantly push him away because I'm scared of getting hurt.

I've now excepted my past mistakes; I am to blame. So, moving forward, I'm trying to change, be a better person, be more chilled, and more considerate with fewer strops. When people are willing to change or to try harder, it means they want a relationship to work.

Perhaps I was meant to endure all difficult chapters, to end up where I was meant to be, in the arms of a loving, caring man. It's time that I got my happy ever after.

42.
ANOTHER STUPID MISTAKE

If you want to find out who's a true friend, screw up then
see who sticks around."
— Karen Salmonsohn

2019…

My life was back on track! Simon made me optimistic about my future. Then I made another stupid mistake!

After telling my friends that the old Vicki was back; that I had this new love in my life; I screwed up again! The mistake nearly ended my life, got me a night in a prison cell, and cost me around £10.000 in fines and vehicle damage.

~

The night in question was February 8, 2019. Mum had told me John was going on a weekend break with our entire friendship group, which included two of my former best friends, Veronica and Anna, who I had supported through thick and thin.

It hurt. I never even received an invitation (not that I would have gone). After our separation, they avoided me like the plague. Nobody gave a shit about how I felt; they preferred to party and get pissed with John as if I were dead. It hurt. I wondered how they would feel if the shoe was on the other foot, and they were the ones being abandoned?

Call me old-fashioned, but I believe you should always put yourself in someone else's position and see how your actions would affect them. I know for a fact, each of my friends would have felt as though they had been kicked to the curb like trash.

~

I had been fighting a winter cough when Anna invited me over for a Prosecco or two. Soon, one bottle turned into three. I'd also been coughing all day and took some dreadful tasting cough syrup, which caused me to lose my appetite. I had eaten almost nothing in 24 hours.

The following evening, Simon called to invite me for an early drink at his local pub. Cold or no cold, food or no food, I was going to see Simon. I figured he would make my blues go away. I drank red wine, unaware that two 175ml glasses puts a woman with food in her stomach at her absolute limit.

I told Simon I needed to go home and cook dinner for the kids. He asked if I was okay to drive. I told him, "No worries. I'm fine." At that moment, I had all my wits about me. I was completely unaware of how long alcohol can remain in the body, particularly for someone that weighed less than 50 kilos.

Simon and I kissed goodbye. He had taken my mind off everything, and I had a new spring in my step. He had a way of convincing me that the past was the past and that he was my future. I drove home with a huge smile on my face. Only I never arrived.

The road was very dark. I came to an accident-prone blackspot junction (a place where road accidents regularly occur) half a mile from the pub. I was about to pull out onto the main road when a Japanese people-carrier approached from my right. It all happened so quickly. I felt the car hit my front bumper, ripping off the front of my car. The impact spun my car 360 degrees. Sparks jumped from the dangling bumper. As I spun out of control, I could see the headlights of oncoming cars trying to avoid a head-on collision. Maybe I was overhanging the junction, maybe the other driver was coming down the hill too fast and came around the bend as I pulled out, I'll never really know.

I shoved the gears into reverse and slammed the gas to avoid the oncoming cars and bounced to an abrupt stop in the woods off to the side of the road. My heart was racing. By some miracle, I was still breathing, with just a bump on the head, a scratch on my hand, and two sore knees. All I can say is my guardian angel must have been watching over me because there was no way I should have survived. Shaken, I texted Simon to tell him I'd crashed. He told me to stay calm, and he would find me.

~

The next thing I remember was two men in fluorescent jackets. They were two police officers who happened to be dealing with another collision nearby. They looked at my crushed car, then looked up and down the road. They asked, "Where are you coming from, Madam?"

"Wrington," I answered.

They were amazed. They realized I'd spun 360 across the carriageway. "You're damn lucky to be alive, Madam."

They helped me out of the vehicle, since I was dizzy and dazed. "What were you doing in Wrington?" asked one.

The last thing I was going to do was lie to a policeman. "I'd met my partner for drinks in the pub and was heading home to make dinner for my daughter."

"Willing to take a breathalyser test?"

"No problem," I said, confidently. After all, I only had two small glasses of wine. At that moment, the drinks the day before at Anna's never even entered my mind.

I followed the luminous jackets to their car. I blew confidently into the machine. The policeman stared at the readings, then huddled off to the side. When they returned, one officer said, "Sorry, Madam, but I've got to arrest you for drink driving."

I lost my cool. "There must be some mistake!"

The policemen remained sternly professional. "Madam, your alcohol reading is twice the legal limit! I would suggest you consider a good solicitor." I was stunned.

As the words sunk in, my world unraveled. This could not be happening. I was under arrest for breaking the law. What would Mum and Dad think, and Simon, the kids, and all the others? All I kept repeating to myself, as I sat in the back of the police car on the way to the station, was, "Another stupid Vicki mistake. Another stupid Vicki mistake…Another…."

43.

PRISON SUCKS

"In prison, you get to see who really loves you."
— Suge Knight

2019…

My world was tumbling, I'd ruined everything, and now I'd lost my freedom.

I was desperate to make a toilet stop en route to Patchway Police Station in Bristol; I was curtly refused. The air was thick with silence, broken only by the occasional police update that blared over the radio.

My 20-mile journey to Bristol felt even scarier than the 2,000-mile flight from the Maldives with crazy Robert 50 Shades of Grey.

When we arrived, I was allowed one call. I rang Shelly, who was caring for my daughter, Emily, while Mummy met with Simon. I informed her of my arrest and begged her to care for my children. "Don't panic," said Shelly calmly. "I'll look after the children. I'll tell them that your car has broken down, so you are staying in Wrington with Simon."

"Can you tell Mum and Dad? I'm only allowed one phone call."

All I could think about was the fact I'd nearly left my two kids without a mum, again, and how their record-free Mummy was now a criminal.

~

A kind-faced custody sergeant read my rights and entitlements as I stood trembling. My belongings were taken, and I was made to sign a charge sheet. How ironic! I'd written this exact scene in two of my crime novels, never imagining in my wildest dreams that I would enact it myself for real.

~.

Black and white, that's all I saw, on the floors, walls, and doors. All designed to intimidate prisoners. My God, how it did. Then there was the walk of shame to the cells. I was terrified.

I paused, observing the square box cell before me, complete with a toilet with no seat, a thin mattress on a concrete slab, and a CCTV camera monitoring every move.

The officer ushered me inside, slammed the door. And a jangling of keys in the lock echoed in the door. That sound, that bang, lingered in my head. Fear coursed through me. I was a prisoner. Mummy was behind bars. Would I come out?

I lay on the freezing mattress and pulled the paper-thin blanket over me. I felt like a quivering ice pop. Perhaps it was shock. Prisoners screamed and banged their angry fists on cell doors at all hours. I cried and cried. Minutes felt like hours. My bruised knee and bumped head ached. I was not offered any treatment. After begging, I was given Paracetamol.

It was clear I was staying for the long haul, until I'd been tested again and processed for my DNA for the Police database. I no longer felt human. I'd been stripped of all dignity, being watched on the toilet. I was evidence now, pure and simple. The police would take any sample they required to secure a conviction.

I was tired and hungry, not having eaten in over 24 hours. Cell lights were switched on for observation. Being watched while having a pee was the least of my concerns. I could now face jail time. Every so often, the letterbox peephole would open, eyes would stare. I was offered the odd glass of water and rank builders tea. (strong tea). All I could think about was the shame that I'd brought on my family and how embarrassed I'd feel facing them, and Simon. I even wondered if my stupidity would drive Simon away.

~

The moment of truth arrived. I was marched from my cell to another stark white room with an intoxication machine. I was ordered to complete tests. All I had to do was blow. It sounded simple, and I provided the first reading. Attempts two and three failed. I did not have the puff. I was too shaken and afraid.

The officer delivered a blow, "Fail again, and we will arrest you for failing to provide a specimen." I balled my eyes out. Never would I attempt to evade a police procedure. I'd complied with every step. Due to my distress, I was offered one final chance. It took every inch of fight left in me to try again. Bingo! I succeeded. My only problem, I was still over the legal limit. I'd be held and processed in the morning.

My police-issue flipflops slapped the lino as I was escorted to a forensic suite. If I didn't already feel like a criminal, that cemented it. Mouth swabs were taken, and each fingerprint scanned. Every evidence sample, I'd ever written about, was extracted from me. The only thing lacking was a forensic paper suit.

As if by magic, I was frogmarched through the chamber of horrors; profanities and fists echoing, as I entered my cell to be kept in isolation for hours. I lay down, staring up at the sky window, waiting for night to fade and dawn to break. It felt like years. I begged for the light to be switched off so I could try and sleep but was ignored.

A kind sergeant later agreed, but no sooner had it been switched off, it was back on blinding my eyes. It was clear, they assumed I could harm myself. I pulled the sheet over my head and let my tears flow, wishing I could go back in time and start my life again, or at least that night.

~

A buzz distracted my sorrow. The wall-mounted intercom rang. The duty sergeant had my sister on the line. Never had I felt so relieved to hear a familiar voice. It was only at this moment that I knew both my children were okay and remained unaware of my arrest.

I begged the custody sergeant to call Simon. She said she would see what she could do. He didn't know where I was. All he had was one text saying I'd crashed before the police arrived. Hours later, the intercom rang again. I wept when I heard Simon's voice. I felt shame and relief. Despite us being so early on in our relationship, he was there wanting to support me, a criminal.

He'd been at his wit's end, trying to contact me after arriving to the crash site and discovering I'd been taken. It didn't matter, the police had made contact. He would collect me. It was those words that made me realize I really had found a good man.

~

A police sergeant visited me. I think it was still dark. She asked me if I knew the severity of the charge. I burst into tears again, then asked:

"Am I going to jail?" She smiled and answered: "No". It was comforting. Then she informed me I'd lose my license for around two years due to the collision at the time of the offense. All I could think about was how I would be letting my children down, how I wouldn't be able to drive them to hospital in an emergency or even get them to their clubs.

Two mental health workers freed me from my cell for an interview to ascertain my state of mind. I explained all I endured in the last eight months. They sat transfixed, as though I were a TV drama. "You've pretty much hit rock bottom, haven't you?" one stated. That's when I wept uncontrollably and couldn't stop. She was right, I was at the bottom of a black cave and couldn't see a way out.

~

The duty solicitor Nicola arrived suited and booted. She reminded me of the girl I once was, a professional. It made me realize how my life had changed, and not for the better. This lady had my back. She peered through her chunky black frames, examining marks on my head, asked if I was okay. I shrugged my shoulders. At least I was alive.

I was told bluntly that I was looking at a 24-month ban but they could add additional charges, if they wanted; dangerous driving, or driving without due care and attention. I'd done neither, I was simply struck. She advised me to answer, "no comment." It was up to the police to prove those charges. She also informed me that she'd been told I was one of the nicest people they'd had in custody, and the charging officer felt sorry for me. "Hopefully, they'll be kind."

~

I was questioned as if in a scene from one of my crime novels. I did as I was instructed and answered, "no comment", which made me feel guilty. My solicitor knew best. I held back the tears and bit my tongue. The officer charged me with one count, driving with excess alcohol.

I was released and given a date to attend court and collect my belongings. I walked from the station, free. I did the walk of shame in clothes from the night before, carrying my belongings in a clear bag with a yellow tag. Having fresh air and contact with the outside world felt like I'd won the lottery.

It was freezing as I waited for Simon outside the police station. "Let's stop by the crash site so you can retrieve any belongings you've left behind," he said. When we arrived at the car, he noticed car vultures had already stolen the headlights, the battery, and bumper. "I'll have it towed to my yard.," he said. "It will be safe there."

I made an awkward call to John, informing him of my arrest and the night behind bars, just before he set off on his planned holiday with the children. He assumed the arrest had something to do with another Vicki emotional crisis. Not once did he ask if I was okay!

When John, Matthew and Emily returned, he just stood on the doorstep conveying disgust because I'd ruined my expensive new Mercedes. The kids, on the other hand, embraced me with hugs, they cared; even if he didn't. Telling them that I would not be able to drive, and that I faced court, was humiliating. But we joked they had a criminal for a mum.

I asked John if he'd keep my ordeal to himself. He promised. I also told him I was aware the crash could have hurt the other driver. And I would be eternally grateful to him keeping my ordeal in confidence.

~

Not long after, I discovered John had broken his promise. He had shared all the crash details with the holiday group: Anna, Tom, Veronica, Ryan, and Brittany. The gossip wheel spread quickly. Everyone I met seemed to be aware of the crash and my arrest. I was convinced John believed embarrassing me was a partial punishment for *his* ordeal of having to put up with my erratic behavior.

Being in jail for a day taught me more about criminal incarceration than working as a crime reporter for nine years: *prison really, really sucks!*

44.

COURT HEARING

"Punishment is not for revenge, but to lessen crime and reform the criminal."

— Elizabeth Fry

2019…

It was time to face the music and be punished.

My court hearing for driving under the influence arrived on February 27.

In attendance were my solicitor, Nicola, Mum and Dad, and my friends Nadia and Mary, who had driven one hour and a half with her young baby to be at my side.

John did not attend the sentencing and offered no support. The time I saw last him, his body language projected anger and frustration. He made me feel small—like every problem we ever had was my fault.

Simon offered moral support but didn't attend the proceeding. He didn't want his first meeting with my parents to be in court. While I would have liked him there to hold my hand for moral support, I respected his decision.

I imagined the worst. I was known to security staff from my reporting days. I had to tell the people that trusted me with sensitive information that I was now on the wrong side of the law. My solicitor ushered me upstairs into an interview room. "We need to talk." The tone sounded ominous. As we walked, I couldn't stop crying. The press would have a field day. The headline flashed in my mind: "Crime Writer Commits Crime!"

~

Nicola said, "I need to prepare you for the worst. I just learned another client facing a similar charge, had just had three more charges added as the court proceedings started. The additional charges of dangerous and careless driving alone, could have severe prison consequences."

I nearly passed out and started hyperventilating. Nicola said calmly, "Take a deep breath, remain calm, I want to check to make sure no additional charges have been added to your case."

I fell apart, was trembling, completely petrified. "What if there are additional charges, does that mean I'd face prison time?" I asked tearfully. "It's a possibility."

~

Nicola left me alone for what seemed like an eternity. The walls of the room felt like they were slowly closing in. Soon I would not be able to breathe. I could feel my heart pounding through my chest.

Nicola opened the door. "We're good. We're dealing with just one charge. But you'll probably lose driving privileges for 24 months due to the collision." I just felt numb. Nicola smiled trying to look optimistic to reduce stress level. "Time to go," she said. I knew the drill; I'd been in court many times as a reporter. Thankfully, I was first up, and there were no reporters present.

The usher locked me in the glass dock. That's when I felt like a criminal. I didn't look at my family or friends; I felt ashamed. Court proceedings got underway. Thankfully, the character references from friends, business contacts, and the former town mayor, and my mitigating letter were read in private chambers, not the open court. For the magistrates it would have been like listening to a story about "a life lost."

~

Still, the magistrate told the open court, "Mrs. FitzGerald, I've read the reports about all your recent circumstances; it's clear you've hit rock bottom." The chair of the bench felt sorry for me; I could see it in her eyes. My tears were uncontrollable. It was true. I'd lost everything, including my dignity. I never imagined I'd find myself in this position.

The court was shown pictures of my destroyed car with the shredded front bumper dangling. I was lucky nobody was seriously hurt. The magistrates gave me an 18-month license ban and offered me a drunk driver's course to reduce the ban to 13 months. Tears of joy rolled down my cheeks. Being freed from the glass chamber was like being granted a second chance to pick up the shattered parts of my life and rebuild it. Not being able to transport the children to their clubs was the worst aspect, I didn't care about me.

~

Two weeks later the kids bought me a bike for my birthday. It was the best gift I had ever received. It offered me freedom.

~

Attending the drunk driver's course over three weeks was humbling. Learning how long it takes alcohol to leave your system was instructional. I'd drank quite a bit of Prosecco the night before the crash. It was still in my bloodstream! It's one unit per hour. A typical 75cl bottle of wine at 12% strength, or three pints of 5% lager, takes 11.5 hours minimum to leave the human body! I could have taken a breath test the following day and would still have been over the legal limit without drinking a glass of wine with Simon.

As I sat there, I realized life was about growing. I decided I would try to learn something new each day. It would keep me sane, and maybe help me avoid stupid choices on the rest of my journey through life. I'd also never let a drop of alcohol pass my lips when my license is back. I wouldn't make the same mistake.

There was one saving grace to the sordid affair. My insurance company would pay third party damages to the other driver and the necessary car repairs..... *or so I thought.*

45.

QUICKIE DIVORCE.COM

Don't fight pain; you can't win. Recovery requires you to surrender to win.

— LV Recovery Center

2019…

It was time to leave the past in the past and start life anew. That required a divorce and agreeing custody.

From my standpoint, I had tried to make our marriage work and lost. From John's standpoint, I had done everything I could to make a mess out of our marriage and succeeded.

Despite our difference of opinion, we shared the same goal for our children—a normal upbringing. John wanted to remain a supportive father—emotionally and financially. For me, the children were my legacy, proof that I had done something very right in my life. We agreed to share custody of Matthew and Emily equally and to identify time spent with each. As we quickly discovered, the strategy was the easy part. Implementing the strategy was stressful and complicated because of the kids' activities, John's busy corporate travel schedule, and my need to find quiet time to write.

Our lives revolved around a written schedule. One week I would have the children for four days and three days the next. Each weekend we would take it in turns, depending upon circumstances. Sometimes, John would seek help from my mum and dad (not his!). My parents would always help him; they have loved their grandchildren since the days they were born. His parents have only ever seen their grandchildren three times a year, despite both being retired and living only one and a half hours away! That's something I've never understood, and, as a result, my children do not have a close relationship with them and never will! That's sad, but it's their choice to remain distant.

John and I speak all the time, and we continue to pride ourselves on our amicable separation. It's important for the children to have a happy childhood without arguments. Although matters became more complicated since John found another partner, a 32-year-old single mum with a 16-month-old baby. I fear she may not be the ideal stepmother for my children. Instead of spending the time necessary to build a bond with my children, she tried to buy their affections at an early stage with gifts, something which angered me greatly.

I can understand that John wants to spend time with her and her son. But, to be honest, the situation has made me angry— this total stranger was laying claim to the time and attention I long craved. I also just discovered that John has chosen to quit being a football coach. How ironic. That was the one thing I begged him to do for years when we were married, yet he refused point-blank. Now, in his new happy life with his girlfriend, he has chosen to act at last. That hurts like a knife.

Maybe this second time around will make John more sensitive to the needs every woman has. Sadly, I don't foresee that circumstance because John's work will always be his number one priority. Right now his new partner sees a successful corporate executive who paid for a lavish all-inclusive Egyptian holiday just five months after they began dating.

~

Given the new circumstances, I decided the only solution was a divorce. The truth was, I no longer wanted to be married to John in name only. Oddly, John never picked up my hints. Perhaps he thought my mind was too fragile and that the legal process could give rise to old demons and tip me over the edge again. I know he wanted no part of that trauma in his neat new life. Maybe there were other reasons; I'll never really know.

I called John, "I've filed for a divorce online; the sooner, the better. I don't think there is any way we can rekindle the spark of love." There was silence. "I agree." His answer spoke volumes about our last five years together.

John and I agreed to keep the divorce proceedings amicable and efficient. I had done some research and discovered a service on the internet called *quickiedivorce.com.* The site pitched a £167 Personal Plus divorce with free phone support, fill-in-the-blank forms, and hundreds of satisfied customer reviews.

John was skeptical. I said, "What do we have to lose? We spend that much at restaurants with friends in one evening!"

I had watched friends go through messy divorce filings that took years to resolve and cost thousands of pounds in unnecessary solicitor's fees. I knew I was not emotionally strong enough to take that route, and as John so aptly put it, "We have fond memories of our life together. We should want those to remain."

~

Splitting our assets was more matter of fact.

With John's background in economics, we also agreed there was no point in wasting money on unnecessary financial advisor fees. It was simple. I would remain in the house with the children, and John would keep his pension. Had I chosen to go after his pension, I would have probably been £300k better off at retirement age. But I felt his pension was his; I wouldn't touch it. I just wanted to keep a home over the kid's heads.

Once everything was agreed, I filed the papers in January and we were divorced by August, two days before John's big 40th birthday celebrations.

~

I called John to inform him. "Looks like you'll receive a great birthday gift from me—your divorce," I joked. John didn't seem to find any humor in my comment. In fact, he barely muttered a word when I told him I had his copy of the Decree Absolute. I think he just didn't know what to say.

While I no longer wanted to be married, I was still devastated and cried for hours. It was the end of an era. I'd spent half of my life with John, and a single piece of paper told me that it was over for good. I felt a range of emotions that day: utter sadness and remorse mixed with a hint of excitement that somewhere out there was a new life with a happy ending.

The old undisciplined Vicki was gone; a new, improved Vicki was on the horizon.

46.

EEKS! ANOTHER LAWSUIT.

> "It's funny how sometimes the people you'd take a bullet for, are the ones behind the trigger."
>
> — Anonymous

2019…

One court case was over, and another was looming on the horizon. I just didn't know it.

Gramps taught me one never betrays a good friend. I've tried to live my life that way. But bad things seem to keep on happening to me.

Life was moving forward after the court case and driving ban; I was surviving. Six weeks later, an envelope arrived in the post. It contained legal papers. I was being sued out of the blue, for up to £10K, by one of my ex-best friends, Lara, over the incident that took place *two years prior.*

Stunned didn't even cut it. My hands shook, and I wanted to vomit when I scrutinized the court summary. I'd thought Lara would never go through with her scheme and fraudulently claim against my car insurance company. I was wrong.

According to the claim, Lara was suing my insurance company for medical damages and the treatment of emotional trauma. She was not even injured. How could she lie?

Admittedly, our friendship was over the moment she broke my trust and told Anna about Mark. I'd always kept her secrets—that's what friends do. Betrayal is the worst feeling anyone can experience. It feels as though you've been punched in the gut. But to go through with a false claim, two years down the road was unbelievable.

I text Lara, saying I was her best friend and asked how she could treat me like that. Her response was cold: "It's just something I've got to do."

I did not believe she would stoop so low. I don't think I ever really knew the real Lara. Perhaps I blinded by the new, exciting friendship? Anna and Lara came as a pair when I'd met Anna. We molded into a trio. I suppose I went with the flow, and it's nice to make new friends.

But as I sat there looking at the paperwork, I wondered whether my 'friend radar' was also broken, just like my boyfriend back in my youth.

As I write this and reflect, I realize I'm naïve and not a good judge of character. I take people at face value, see the positives in them, not the flaws. That trait is my weakness and going forward, after being betrayed by Lara, Anna, and Veronica, I've huge barriers up. I won't let just anyone in my life anymore. I've learned one of the hardest lessons in life: *friends can hurt and betray you.*

I immediately informed the insurance company that it was a false claim. Subsequently, the company hired a private investigator. I had to provide a detailed witness statement, which included photos of Lara and I socializing in the immediate aftermath and long after the incident. They judged the claim to be fraudulent and refused to pay the damages. The matter would go to court.

In the last conversation I had with the solicitors, appointed by my car insurance company, they said that Lara's evidence had been submitted. In their view, it was a 50/50 case, and either one of us could win. They found that troubling and wondered whether they should settle out of court to avoid court costs.

I told them I was unhappy with their point of view, but at the end of the day, it was their decision to make, not mine. Should it come to that, I will have to face my ex-best friend in courtroom—despite nursing her through a separation, cooking dinners, taking her kids to school when she was incapable. How ironic!

47.
STILL STANDING

"I'm still standing after all this time. Looking like a true survivor, feeling like a little kid."

— Elton John

2019…

With my children by my side, life is good.

It's hard to believe I'm only 38. With a little luck, I have another 50 years or so to get it right! After everything I've endured; pain, betrayal, tragedy, and near death, I'm *still standing*. Don't ask me how or why. I don't have the answers, just questions.

Why did John get to keep the old life?

Why did those I adored choose sides, and walk away from me?

Why hadn't bad karma punished my millionaire monster?

Is God done punishing me?

Where do I go from here?

Have I been thrown a lifeline?

Will writing continue to be a major part of my life?

I don't have the answers, just hopes, wishes, and dreams. I plan to take each day as it comes and try to make myself happy. I've tried the alternative three times, and I'm certain that's not the answer.

I have laid my soul bare as therapy for my soul and to help others who are struggling. In my mind, getting my story down on paper has eased my pain. I assume some people will judge, criticize, and scorn me for my brutal honesty. But it was my decision, one that I do not regret. I feel rejuvenated, as though a weight's been lifted.

I've gone from a normal life to experience depression, drugging, assault at the hands of Mr. Millionaire (aka Robert), a frightening encounter with the law, lost freedom, the judicial system, divorce, and multiple suicide attempts.

I hope my struggle to survive inspires at least one person at rock bottom to keep climbing, keep swimming and hold their head above water when they're drowning. The message is simple: *if I can weather the storm until the sun shines again, so can you!*

~

Unfortunately, there are still painful battles to face.

My former friend Lara for one. I will have to attend court to give evidence against her fraudulent £10k claim for personal injury that she never sustained. How could a friend do that to another? If she wins, I know my insurers will pay her claim, but it's the principle that matters. Why should she get awarded £10k when she was dancing and drinking just days after the crash?

There is also another matter of the third-party damage claim from my Mercedes crash. My insurers had reassured me that damages to the other party would be paid. Six months later, I was informed they'd made a mistake and told if I didn't refund the funds paid to the third-party (£18k), they'll seek legal remedies. It terrifies me that I could be paying that reimbursement until the day I die, or I win the lottery. I'm sure there is no chance in hell John will help despite our 17 years.

And there are those that will be unhappy because I've named names and shared my secrets. I've been told: "You're a disgusting disgrace and should be ashamed for sharing your suicidal tendencies with anyone." Privately, I wonder if this may be down to embarrassment or guilt for not being more supportive when I desperately needed a helping hand.

One of my priorities is to let go of my bitterness, disappointment, resentment toward those I loved, those who let me down. I'm genuinely excited about the prospect of living happily ever after; however, one chooses to define that.

Another priority is to live every day to the fullest. I'm no longer ashamed to admit I've made some REALLY BIG mistakes. But it no longer matters. As Simon often reminds me, "Vicki, it doesn't matter if you're down or upset, that's life. You cannot change anything; you just have to deal with it."

He's right. I was ill, and now I'm better.

Most importantly, both of my children say I am brave to share my story; they are proud of their Mum. That alone makes this endeavor worthwhile.

~

I'm also at peace with the collateral damage I've created. The breakup with John has caused a custodial time split. I miss my children terribly when they are not here. Emily and Matthew are a blessing. They continue to brighten every day. I love them beyond words.

The fact that John remains part of my family leaves me sad and disappointed. All I want is for Mum and Dad to understand better what happened to their Vicki and to love me without reservation. My feeling is my actions so confused matters that I know it will take time for me to re-earn their trust. I want Mum and Dad to be as proud of me as they once were.

Just spending time with Simon reminds me there is a future waiting for me. But I'm what the Americans call high maintenance—not knowing how life next pages will turn out petrifies me.

I'm hoping God has finally decided I've been punished enough and have been given a lifeline.

~

Friends. I've also learned with certainty that no one should go through life without them. True friends are as important as family and partners. While I've more than I imagined, two girls stand out above all the rest.

Mary practically jumped on my chest and fought to keep my heart beating when I'd given up and lost all hope. She was my personal lifeguard who pulled my lifeless body from life's choppy waters.

She's an angel sent from heaven disguised as a friend, who has stood by my side for twenty years supporting me through the bad, rejoicing at the good, and has loved me when I didn't love myself. Our friendship is worth more than treasure, and the thought of not having her in my life is unbearable. I know we will have each other's backs until we are grey and old.

And, then there is Gina, who, despite her divorce proceedings, has been a shoulder of comfort—we're two broken women trying to fix each other. I'm not sure we will ever be completely fixed, but fate has rekindled our friendship to guide us through turmoil and heartache. I adore her and feel blessed she is in my life. Again, she will remain an important and cherished fixture in my life.

As I learned when I was down and out, it's not grand gestures that count, it's the simple things that make a huge difference. The daily inspirational quotes from Marshall, the check-in messages from Ian, Louise, Kylie, and, of course, the hugs, cups of tea, and the wine from Andy when I'm having a particularly rough time. Then there are the Prosecco girls, Aida and Brigita, and the fabulous adventures they take me on to keep me smiling. Every one of them, and of course, my family, are the reason I'm still standing. Together, their support is strengthening my resilience to keep on going, get myself back on my feet, and to achieve my dreams as an established author.

Chronicling my journey has made me an unlikely new friend. The acclaimed American author, M.G. Crisci—his real name is Mathew—he lives 6,000 miles away.

We had a chance meeting at the 2018 Dublin Writer's Conference where I pitched a film treatment for my novel, *Kill List*, to the noted Hollywood producer Ken Atchity, in front of 50 other contestants. Nervous and insecure, I bombed. One year later, I reconnected with Matt at the same conference. We agreed it was time to pitch my novel to Ken again. We polished the treatment and rehearsed my pitch. And I decided to throw caution to the wind. When the competition was over, one treatment was selected for further script development—mine!

It was that one moment I'd dreamed of, and I celebrated in style with Mathew. Being chosen was the boost I'd needed. Timid, shy, insecure Vicki stepped forward and whispered confidently, "I'm ready, it's time." We agreed to tell my story.

I told Mathew bits of my roller-coaster ride through life. That was the birth of *Standing Still*. As I bared my soul over the next 12 months, Mathew begged for more truth. I dug deeper. His constant refrain: why, why, why? During our unique collaboration, I did something I've not done before: I revealed all my secrets. In the process, I came to trust him without reservation. Professionally, he has polished every word of this book. In doing so, he has helped me polish my life. We are and shall remain friends forever.

Perhaps, I am more loved than I ever thought possible. Life doesn't give us second chances often; I'm going to make the most of it and ensure I give back.

The other day my dad made me the proudest woman in the whole world. He told me he loved me "without reservation." And that he would support anything I wanted to do—including publishing this book to wipe the slate clean.

I'm also happy to report that my black widow veil has vanished. I realize I do deserve to be happy. I feel loved, adored, and cherished. Most important, I am still standing, because sometimes, life just happens.

48.
FINAL VICTORY

"God gives never those he loves, more little tests than they can handle."

— Arthur Mercado

2020…

Sometimes, plans just change.

Originally, chapter 47 was going to be the end of *Still Standing*. But, as you've read, my life doesn't work that way. With the loss of my driver's license in chapter 43, I had to do a workaround for transportation. So, with a new bike, I tooled around town for ten months. I was approaching Christmas and 2020, looking forward to a new start.

Mary visited for a weekend. We ate Japanese and enjoyed a lovely girl's catch up. She confirmed that my smile had been restored and said she felt happy that I'd come through my battles.

"I've got my Vicki back," Mary declared, face beaming.

"You're right. I feel like myself again, albeit a bit damaged."

"You are not damaged. You have been through some tough ordeals, but look at you, you're a fighter and stronger than ever!"

We smiled at one and other. I felt ecstatic to be enjoying Mary's company and happy that she could see how far I'd come, having crawled back from the depths of despair.

Mary left the next morning, and I spent the afternoon enjoying a Sunday Roast with Simon and playing a few fun games of Spoof and Table Skittles with friends. A smile remained as I returned home, agreeing to do John a favor and care for the children, so he could have an early night and catch an early train to London for work.

~

It soon transpired that John was giving the children back so he could stay overnight with his girlfriend. Understandingly, I was angry and felt used. Had he been honest with me at the outset, I wouldn't have had a problem. It was the fact he lied and was deceitful. A row ensued. I could not understand why he would want to cut short his time with his children, to be with his girlfriend. I regard my allocated time as precious; children don't stay children forever!

The discussion blew out of proportion. John refused to return home and collect the children, choosing his girlfriend over the kids! Upset and angry, I decided to cycle to my parents. Only I was shaken and distressed and not fully concentrating through teary eyes. My bike mounted a curb as I tried to negotiate onto the pavement. I fell off and crashed to the floor.

Fuelled with adrenalin, I got back up and tried to pedal away, only my leg turned to jelly and I collapsed with shock. There, I lay crying unable to move. I called my parents who came to my rescue, as did passers-by, who waited by my side for three hours as the temperature plummeted to -2 degrees (the coldest night of the year). One man lit a chiminea to keep me warm while we waited for the ambulance. Others covered me with their coats, blankets, and a hot water bottle to prevent me from catching hypothermia.

Call handlers informed my father that I was "not a priority" as I was not bleeding or unconscious. Therefore, I was forced to wait for three hours with no pain relief. Instead, caring angels knelt beside me told me to squeeze their hands. I'll never forget them!

After being administered gas and air and admitted to The Bristol Royal Infirmary, it was clear my leg was banana-shaped. My foot and knee were pointing in opposite directions. X-rays confirmed NINE spiral fractures to my fibula and tibia.

"Vicki, your injury is very serious. This is the worst x-ray I've ever seen," a nurse declared. "Would you like to look?" she added.

"No, thanks."

I was taken back to the ward, given an anesthetic to sedate me while the reduction was carried out to straighten the bones. My leg was plastered and x-rayed a second time. It remained badly twisted. The plaster cast was cut off and I was sedated again. Torsion continued and I was plastered and x-rayed again.

"It's much better than it was, though you will still require surgery. A metal rod will be inserted through your knee to stabilize and repair the fractures," a doctor confirmed.

"It hurts so much," I replied.

"I'm not surprised; this is significant trauma, but rest assured, we can fix it and get you walking again."

I was scheduled for surgery the following afternoon, after a CT scan, but an emergency pushed me down the list. I had to wait another 24 hours until I went under the knife.

"You'll be up and walking the day after we insert the rod," the doctor promised.

It sounded promising. Only, the pain was horrific, and I was bleeding. I begged for a doctor to come at 10 PM, but help never arrived. At 1 AM, saturated in blood, I pressed the alarm button. A doctor removed the bandages and discovered the surgeons had left two open wounds from the wire entry points. Had I not woken, I could have bled to death.

Physiotherapists made me walk less than 24-hours later. Every step was excruciating. That exercise resulted in massive swelling to the point I begged nurses for help in the middle of the night.

"Please, cut the bandages off. They're hurting. My leg is so swollen," I begged. "I need more morpheme; the pain's unbearable." Fortunately, the nurse cut off the bandages and provided ice to reduce the swelling. I kept my leg on ice for much of the following day feeling utterly miserable, until I received an exciting, surprise email.

It was from Ken Atchity, the publisher of Story Merchant Books, a respected American publisher I had met at the most recent Dublin Conference. He said, "My team and I reviewed the film treatment of your exciting thriller, *Kill List*. The treatment is solid, and I think quite commercial. Also, if *Kill List* hasn't been published, I'd be pleased to represent the property."

I smiled; *the music hadn't died!*

Ken's news gave me a new impetus to heal quickly. The nurse explained the protocol: I would be discharged once I'd mastered the stairs. With every ounce of energy and determination, I clenched my teeth and climbed the rehab stairs on day six.

"I'm more than satisfied that you can go home," the physio declared, face smiling.

I was beyond happy. I wanted to go home so much it brought a tear to my eye. I needed my children, my family, and my man, Simon. For five days, I'd laid on my back staring at the ceiling, only moving to use the bedpan. Being in Bristol made it difficult for people to visit. I'd felt lost, lonely and afraid. Yet, I was still here after winning another battle with exciting prospects on the horizon.

After this latest roller-coaster ride, I am confident that I can overcome whatever *little tests* life continues to throw my way.

I'm a fighter.

I'm stronger than ever—to hell with crutches and opioids.

I'm no quitter. I never give up.

I'm still standing! And, I always will.

AFTERWORD

"Time to lock and load. Time to get control.
Time to search the soul and start again."

— Bob Seeger

Now and Forever...

Vicki FitzGerald is, quite simply, a magnificent woman. She has been through many doors in her short life. She has given me the honor of walking alongside her as she has returned from the brink and now thrives in the sunshine.

The reader may wonder why this book. Vicki is not a celebrity, just a woman trying to make her way through what we call life. And, the circumstances have left her a bit shaky.

Call it fate or Irish luck, Vicki and I first met at a writer's conference in Dublin, Ireland. As the father of three sons, I know little about raising girls; my 15-year-old granddaughter will attest to that! Somehow, Vicki and I had instant chemistry. As we talked over tea and such, I discovered behind Vicki's cheery mask sat a tempestuous world of self-doubt wrapped in her life to date. A life that included broken relationships, two children, and numerous emotional and physical challenges.

I suggested her story, told correctly, could touch people's hearts, perhaps even offer some life lessons without being preachy.

She said politely, "No, thank you."

One year later, we met again in Dublin, this time over a pint. I said nothing of our prior conversation. Eyes twinkling like two bright stars, Vicki nodded, "I'm good now. It's time."

The process of converting the circumstances of Vicki's life into a literary work with purpose was challenging. It required soulful retrospection, an unshakeable willingness to collaborate, and a friendship built on mutual trust. During that year, I probably got to know her better than any woman, other than my wife, Mary Ann, who took me on some 50+ years ago.

One year later, Vicki and I were staring at a raw, honest draft of Vicki's soul on paper. It's hard to put into words how we felt at that moment. We just hugged and smiled. Then came the struggles, should I, or shouldn't I? From what I can tell, the naysayers far outnumbered the yeasayers.

Not everyone will agree with the choices Vicki has made, but all my instincts, as a writer and a father, tell me that her story is one you will not soon forget. It contains lessons for everyone, regardless of age and circumstance.

And, to all those people who did not support her in her darkest moments, I am sad for you. But none of that matters anymore, she is well, feisty as ever, and has vowed to live the rest of her life in the sunshine. I believe her. I applaud her. I love her like my own daughter.

Request for Review

Dear Reader,

We want to thank you for taking the time to read our book.

We realize *Still Standing* is somewhat unconventional, and we know you have many choices. We have tried to do everything we could to create a book that entertains and informs, a book you will not soon forget.

We recognize everybody lives busy lives these days, but we would appreciate you posting a short review with the retailer from which you purchased *Still Standing*. It will help other readers to discover my library of 13 books.

If you'd like to join my monthly mailing list, there's an interesting free book offer on my website www.mgcrisci.com, or learn more about me, put ***mg crisci*** into your google search bar.

Thanks again. See you somewhere along the way.

M. G. Crisci

Printed in Great Britain
by Amazon